• HALSGROVE DISCOVER SERIES ➤

THE NORFOLK COAST

ALAN CHILDS AND DONALD MACKENZIE
MAPS BY ASHLEY SAMPSON

HALSGROVE

First published in Great Britain in 2005
Reprinted 2008
Copyright © 2005 Alan Childs and Donald MacKenzie
Maps by Ashley Sampson

Dedicated to our parents

Disclaimer
While the authors have walked all the routes described in the book, no responsibility can be
accepted for any omissions or errors or for any future changes that may occur in the details given.
The authors and publisher cannot accept any liability for accident, mishap or loss arising from the use of this book.

British Library Cataloguing–in–Publication Data
A CIP record for this title is available from the British Library

ISBN 978 1 84114 428 3

HALSGROVE
Halsgrove House
Ryelands Industrial Estate, Bagley Road,
Wellington Somerset TA21 9PZ
Tel: 01823 653777
Fax: 01823 216796
email: sales@halsgrove.com
website: www.halsgrove.com

Printed and bound by D'Auria Industrie Grafiche Spa, Italy

Contents

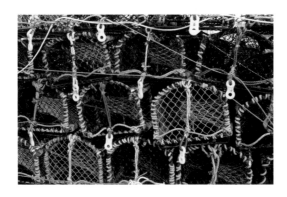

Photo Credits

Alan Childs: cover; title page; contents tl, cl, bl, cr; br; p4; p5; p6; p7; p8; p9; p12 t; p13 c&b; p14; p15; p16; p17; p18; p19; p20; p21 bl&r; p22; p.24; p31 t; p32; p34; p35 t; p36; p39; p40 t; p41; p42; p43 b; p44; p46 b; p47; p48 l&br; p49; p50; p51 t; p52; p53 b; p54; p55; p56 t; p57; p58; p62 t; p64; p65; p66; p67; p68 tl&bl; p69 b; p70; p71 t; p72; p73; p74 b; p75; p76 l&bl; p78 t; p80 b; p82 t. p83 br; p84 b; p86; p87; p88; p89; p90; p91 l; p92; p93; p95 bl; p97; p99; p101; p102 b; p104 b; p105; p106; p107 b; p108 b; p109 b; p110; p111 b; p114 t; p120 b; p121; p122; p128 t&b; p129 tr&br; p130 r; p140 b; p142 b; p144;

Sarah Childs: p40 b; Ken Durrant: p91 r; Wendy George: p46 t; Simon Harrap: p120 t; Dave Hawkins: p48 tr; Harold Hems: p12 b; p35 bl&br; p45 t; p51 b; p69 t; p80 tl&cl; p94 l; p119; p134; Dave Horsley: p33; Tony Howes: p59t; p77 t; p102 t; p103 b; p109 t; p127 b; p141 t; Tony Leech: p53 r; p127 t; p133 tr;

Donald MacKenzie: contents tr; p21 tl; p25; p26; p27; p28; p29; p30; p31 b; p38; p56 b; p60; p61; p76 tr&br; p77 b; p78 c&b; p79 l&tr; p81 l&br; p82 b; p83 t&bl; p84 t; p94 t; p95 t&br; p96; p98; p104 t; p107 t; p108 t; p111 t; p112; p113; p114 b; p115; p116; p117; p123; p124; p125; p126; p129 bl; p130 l; p131; p133 l&br; p135; p136; p137; p138; p139; p140 t; p141 b; p142 t; p143;

Ashley Sampson: p13 t; p45 b; p62 b; p71 b; p74 t; p79 br; p81 tr; p103 t; Colin Turner: p68 r; C. Hans Watson: p43 t.

NOTE: t=top; c=centre; b=bottom; tr=top right etc etc.

Acknowledgements

Ms J. Allen (Gressenhall); Mr K. Arnott; Mr and Mrs N. Ashton; Mr P. Brooks; Burnley Hall Estate Office; Mr R. Brown; Churches Conservation Trust (St Nicholas Chapel, King's Lynn); Mr P. Crichton (and Hunstanton lifeboat crew); Mr and Mrs M. Chesterman (and staff of 'Ship Inn', Brancaster); Mrs J. Clover; Mrs C. Driscoll; Eastern Counties Newspapers Library staff; Mr A. Fakes; Ms N. Gale; Mrs Harrup; Headteacher and Governors of Sidestrand Hall School; Mrs M. Heather; Mr H. Hems FRPS; Mr G. Hibberd; Holkham Hall Estate Office; Mr R. Hornigold; Mr D. Horsley; Lord Howard of Rising; Mr and Mrs J. Howells; Mr T. Howes; Mr and Mrs B. Howling; Mrs O. Isherwood; Mrs B. Kerrison; Mrs S. Landale; Mr K. Lawson; Dr. A. Leech; Le Strange Estate Office; Mr B. Locke; Mr and Mrs T. Meredith; Norfolk Coast Partnership; Major J. Perkins; Mrs A. Powell (The Pleasaunce CE Holiday Centre); Mrs P. Rhoades (warden) and the ladies of Trinity Hospital, Castle Rising; Mr P. Riney (and the staff of RSPB Titchwell); Royal West Norfolk Golf Club; Mr A. Sampson; Sandringham Estate Office; Mr R. Shipp; Mr. P. Stibbons; Mr and Mrs C. Stockton; Mr G. Storey; Ms W. Sycamore (Borough Council of King's Lynn and West Norfolk; Dr M. Taylor; TIC staff in all local offices; Mr and Mrs R. Thurston; Mr D. Waite MVO, Hon. Clerk to the Trustees, Trinity Hospital Castle Rising; Mr. M. Warren; Wash Estuary Project; Mr. H. Watson; Mr and Mrs M. Welland; Mr L. West; Mr G. Wildridge.

We express our sincere thanks to the priests in charge and the church wardens of the following parish churches: Terrington St Clement; St Margaret, King's Lynn; St.Lawrence, Castle Rising; St Mary, Snettisham; St Mary, Old Hunstanton; St Margaret, Burnham Norton; All Saints, Burnham Thorpe; St Mary, Burnham Deepdale; St Clement, Burnham Overy; St Nicholas, Wells; St John, Stiffkey; St Nicholas, Blakeney; St Margaret of Antioch, Cley; St Nicholas Salthouse; All saints, Upper Sheringham; St Michael and All Angels, Sidestrand; All Saints, Walcott; Holy Trinity Winterton; St Nicholas, Great Yarmouth.

Authors' Note

It is an impossible task to do justice to the many strands that make up the story of the Norfolk Coast; we are aware that our selections of what to include are tokens of a much wider whole. Norfolk birds deserve, and indeed have received, full treatment elsewhere, as has the county's flora. Likewise there are more detailed surveys of its history, including for example, the richness of its medieval churches, over 600 in this county, with more round-towers than in any other. What has been possible is an introduction to the fascinating array of villages and towns abutting the coast. It is hoped that the 'things to do' sections will be helpful in pointing visitors to Norfolk in the right direction. Plants and birds have been included at appropriate places, especially the common examples. Where pubs or hotels are mentioned, they are personal choices: there are others equally good that have not been included. Basic phone numbers have been given and are correct at the time of publication. Most tourist venues and pubs have their own web sites which can be called up by a general search. The walks suggested have tended to be manageable family-oriented strolls through beautiful unspoilt coastal countryside rather than lung-bursting hikes, but there is a number of longer walks already available for the more serious walkers. And of course the Norfolk Coastal Path has been in place since 1986. It gives a challenge of 47 miles, from Hunstanton to Cromer, 36 of these miles through Sites of Special Scientific Interest (SSSI) designated areas. The 'National Cycle Route' No. 1 covers part of north-west Norfolk from King's Lynn to Holkham, and onwards inland. So enjoy all that the coast has to offer - and potter rather than rush. Note well the beautiful combination of Norfolk orange pantiles with rugged grey flints in the architecture of the villages, and the trees along the field edges bowing away from the prevailing winds; enjoy the summer swathes of sea lavender, and the fresh saltiness of sea air. Leave the car behind and get out onto the marshes and dunes, along the recommended tracks, and re-charge the human batteries under Norfolk's gloriously wide-open skies.

A busy summer's beach scene at West Runton with families enjoying the breakers.

Introduction

There is something for everyone along Norfolk's coast. Ornithologists, botanists, geologists and historians target the area, as do 'ordinary' tourists including yachtsmen (and women), and beach-lovers of all ages. Along its cliffs and within its sand dunes, its saltmarshes and muddy tidal estuaries, are rich varieties of animal, bird and plant life. For Norfolk's birdlife in particular, superlatives seem to apply. North Norfolk has been called 'the bird-watching capital of Britain'. Titchwell is the country's most visited Royal Society for the Protection of Birds (RSPB) reserve. Cley was the first county Wildlife Trust, inaugurating the national movement. It is today held to be one of the UK's premier bird-watching sites. Blakeney Point has seabird colonies of national importance. The Wash is a wetland of international importance (as designated following the Ramsar Convention). There are six coastal National Nature Reserves in the county. The Winterton Dunes (one of the largest in the UK) are the home for a wide range of both breeding and overwintering birds and also the rare nattterjack toad. And so it goes on.

History abounds in the villages and towns of the coastland area: from King John's disastrous encounter with The Wash, to George Vancouver setting sail from King's Lynn; from Lord Nelson, whose early sailing lessons were in the area of his home at Burnham Thorpe, to the pioneering agriculturalist Coke of Holkham; from the Roman pedigree of Brancaster to the amazing treasure hoard at Snettisham. At a simpler level, there have been the centuries of making the tides yield a living for the ordinary folk in the villages bordering the North Sea. And of course even the most unlikely people took advantage of an illicit delivery from a 'gentleman of the night', including it is said, the first Prime Minister Robert Walpole (MP for King's Lynn 1702-42) living at his Norfolk home at Houghton. Even the respectable Parson Woodforde had an arrangement with a local smuggler! It sometimes seems that smuggling was a national industry – certainly a well-developed Norfolk one. The history of Norfolk's coastal ports has also been one of constant change. In the Middle Ages there were groups of thriving harbours, such as the so-called 'Glaven ports' around Cley, which were eventually choked of their deep water. Towns and villages have also succumbed over the centuries and are now the stuff of legends, ghostly church bells being heard beneath the waves.

The Norfolk coast, from King's Lynn in the west to Great Yarmouth in the east, is an area of rich diversity and unique habitats. It is not surprising that sections of this unspoilt

Late afternoon sky near Salthouse.

Sunset behind Weybourne mill.

coastland have been designated Areas of Outstanding Natural Beauty (AONB), from 1968. In addition the category SSSI helps to protect particularly sensitive areas. The designation 'Heritage Coast' supports the protection of the 'wildness' so characteristic of this coastland. But it is also a fragile environment where man-made or natural disasters, such as the catastrophic 1953 Floods, can cause problems from which some species of fauna or flora may never recover. There is a fine balance between reasonable access for the human species and the protection of others. Plant life is so often crucial in establishing the build up of protective sand and mud. The power of the North Sea in all its fury is formidable and the dunes, the cliffs and marshes are extremely vulnerable. 'Foreign' granite boulders, so-called 'rock armour', have been added to selected sites to lessen the impact of the waves, and wooden and concrete defences have all been tried. But with global warming, and scientific predictions of a rise in sea level, the future both for property-owners, especially in the east, and for the many reserves along large stretches of the county's shoreline is a frightening one. Action groups have been called into being to monitor the future of their communities if sea defences are not maintained. There is also a complex working-together of organisations and agencies to support the future of this remarkable coastline. The Norfolk Coast Partnership, funded by national and local government acts as a co-ordinating agency.

Man's dependence upon the sea has also changed, and many adjustments have had to take place in the local fishing industries, for example. A small town such as Sheringham had more than 200 fishing boats at its height in the 19th century, and today has a mere handful. The same story would be reflected in other towns and villages along the coast. Although agriculture remains significant to the area, and other sources of income have fallen into place, such as food processing, light-engineering and joinery and a variety of financial and professional services, tourism has of course largely helped to fill the gap. Our towns and their people have quite rightly taken advantage of Norfolk's rich heritage and diversity. It is an area well worth exploring, and it is hoped this book will whet the appetite for many a visit to this very special corner of England.

1 – The Wash Area

There is something more than space or light, something more than weather or seasons. There is history as well as geography. Every field, bridge, tree, house and church has its own history. Everything the eye can see is there for a reason.
(Edward Storey, *Spirit of the Fens*)

There is a primordial quality about this wetland corner of Norfolk, as it borders the next county of Lincolnshire. It was once a thick forest linking us to mainland Europe. It has its own untamed character, giving the impression that man has made little impact on it. King John misjudged it badly when he sent his baggage wagons on a shorter route, and the marshes could still so easily set a trap for the unwary. There are wide vistas and seemingly inadequate banks to hold back the waters. The Romans were possibly the first to build retaining banks, although the so-called 'Roman Bank' is in all likelihood a misnomer. Over the centuries the battle has continued. During the Middle Ages, the area was very prosperous agriculturally with a string of rich Fenland villages, and a thriving wool trade. During the mid 17th century Dutch engineers under Vermuyden were responsible for constructing the Old and New Bedford Rivers in an attempt to drain the Fens. During the First World War, German prisoners provided necessary labour on The Wash embankments. Two artificial islands, part of an abortive Wash barrage sheme, can still be seen.

Equine (over age!) drinkers are encouraged at this pub in Walpole Cross Keys, near the county boundary.

The area contains many fine churches such as that of Terrington St Clement, aptly described as the 'Cathedral of the Marshes'. Because of the problems of obtaining sufficiently strong foundations in this marshy region, the tall tower was built alongside the church rather than on the church itself. Among its former rectors was Edmund Gonville, of Gonville and Caius fame. When in the 17th century the villagers of Terrington St Clement were in danger from the floods, another rector carried his parishioners on his back to safety. They sheltered in the church tower, and were fed by supplies brought from King's Lynn by boat. In the village is Lovell's Hall, Norman in origin but rebuilt in Tudor times by Sir Thomas Lovell, Chancellor of the Exchequer to Henry VIII. Another historic link in the area is that the Prince of Orange (later William III) stayed in Terrington as the guest of Baron Feagle, a refugee from the Netherlands.

'The cathedral of the marshes'.

Terrington Marshes to Heacham

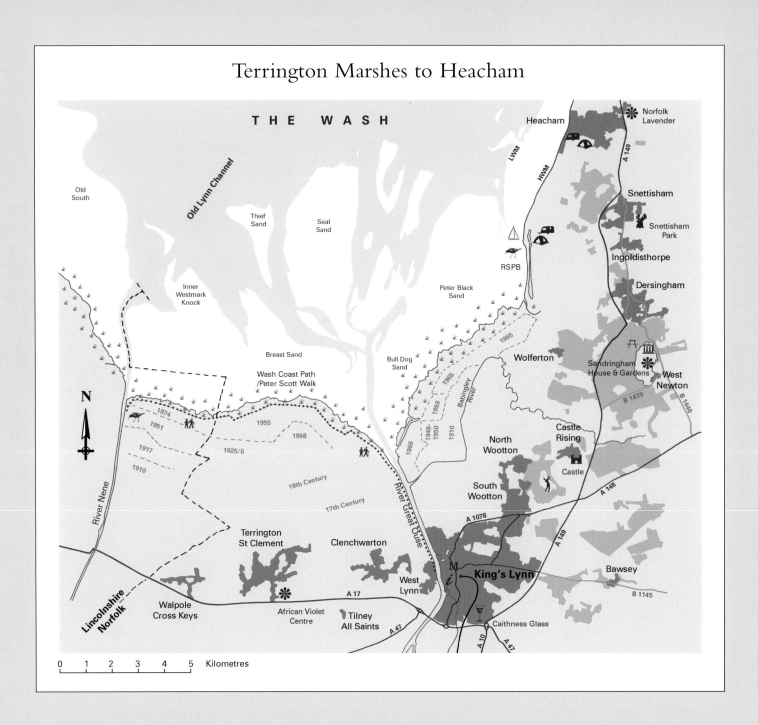

THE WASH

Norfolk Lavender

Heacham

Old South

Old Lynn Channel

Snettisham

LWM

HWM

A 149

Thief Sand

Seal Sand

Snettisham Park

Ingoldisthorpe

Inner Westmark Knock

RSPB

Peter Black Sand

Dersingham

N

Breast Sand

Wash Coast Path /Peter Scott Walk

Bull Dog Sand

Wolferton

Sandringham House & Gardens

West Newton

1965

Babingley River

B 1439

1974

1951

1955

1868

1948

1950

1910

North Wootton

Castle Rising

Castle

1917

1925/6

1910

18th Century

1966

River Great Ouse

South Wootton

A 148

17th Century

A 1078

River Nene

Terrington St Clement

Clenchwarton

A 149

Bawsey

West Lynn

M

i

King's Lynn

B 1145

Lincolnshire
Norfolk

Walpole Cross Keys

African Violet Centre

A 17

Tilney All Saints

A 47

A 10

A 47

Caithness Glass

0 1 2 3 4 5   Kilometres

Key to coastal maps

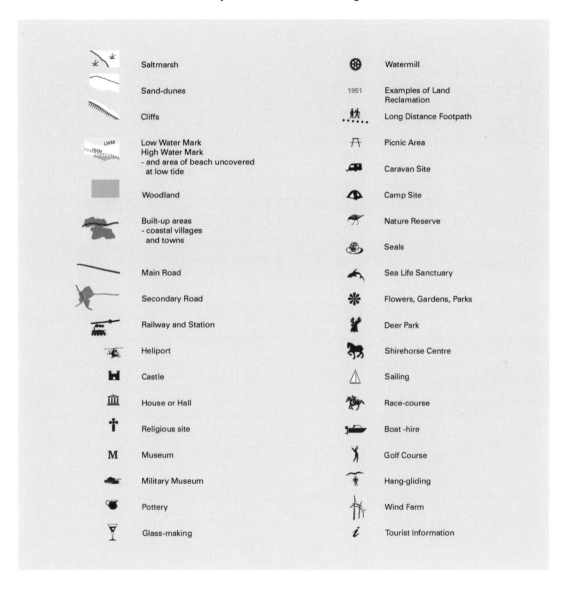

	Saltmarsh			Watermill
	Sand-dunes		1951	Examples of Land Reclamation
	Cliffs			Long Distance Footpath
	Low Water Mark High Water Mark - and area of beach uncovered at low tide			Picnic Area
	Woodland			Caravan Site
	Built-up areas - coastal villages and towns			Camp Site
				Nature Reserve
	Main Road			Seals
	Secondary Road			Sea Life Sanctuary
	Railway and Station			Flowers, Gardens, Parks
	Heliport			Deer Park
	Castle			Shirehorse Centre
	House or Hall			Sailing
	Religious site			Race-course
	Museum			Boat -hire
	Military Museum			Golf Course
	Pottery			Hang-gliding
	Glass-making			Wind Farm
				Tourist Information

The wide open expanses of The Wash, looking towards distant Lincolnshire.

The dunlin visits Britain for the winter. Large flocks fly in close formation and 10,000 have been estimated at a high tide roost on The Wash.

THE AFRICAN VIOLET CENTRE

A German Government official, and an enthusiastic botanist, Baron Walter Von St Paul was the first to record the wild African violets in Tanganyika (now Tanzania). He sent specimens back to Germany where they were grown successfully. The new plant was called Saintpaulia in his honour and given the specific epithet 'ionantha' (violet-flowered). It is not however related to the British wild violet. Since the 1940s a range of colours has been developed. The African Violet Centre at Terrington was set up in 1973 by the Revd. Tony Clements, and was re-developed in 1999 by Paul Crake and Mark Leach. It is the UK's largest independent African violet nursery, and has been awarded many gold medals at the Chelsea Flower Show since 1987.

Sea purslane is a grey-leaved plant often seen edging the creeks in the saltmarshes.

THE LEGEND OF THE MISTLETOE BOUGH

Lovell's Hall in Terrington St Clement is the possible origin of a strange and tragic story. In its medieval past the story has it that a young bride and her husband were celebrating their wedding. After the feasting, the girl decided on a game of hide and seek. Clutching a sprig of mistletoe she ran to a far corner of a dusty attic and found a suitably large chest in which to hide. The complicated lock engaged when the lid was closed and the girl was imprisoned. Frantic searches for her were to no avail. After some days the stricken bridegroom shut up the house and departed. Years later it is said, he returned, and one day a chance search of the attics revealed the chest. Inside he found the skeleton of his young bride. The legend (strangely appealing to Victorian sensibilities) was captured in Thomas Haynes Bayley's ballad 'The Mistletoe Bough', and became very popular. And like all good legends, the Lovell Hall story has a ghost. Each Christmas Eve a young girl in bridal white is supposed to walk down from the attics, still clutching her sprig of mistletoe.

An early spring display of multicoloured African violets.

The Wash is considered to be one of the outstanding areas of the country for its wildlife; it is without doubt regarded as the most important area of estuarine mudflat in Britain. Silt has created vast mudflats and saltmarshes that form one of Britain's most important winter feeding grounds. Curlews, godwits, redshanks and sandpipers use their long bills to bore into the mud; there are oystercatchers, turnstones, knot, sanderling, little ringed plover, ringed plover, dunlin and little stint. Large flocks of brent geese, pink-footed geese and widgeon use the area, together with eider duck, shelduck, mallard, smew, goosanders and scoters. The sand banks also support the largest group of common seals in Europe.

It is not surprising that The Wash estuary has been designated an SSSI, and a National Nature Reserve. At the Ramsar Convention in Iran, back in 1971, it was identified as a wetland of international importance. It is also a Special Protection Area because of its importance for migratory species (European Communities Directive of April 1979), and a Special Area of Conservation. Five different designations!

Right: Lovell's Hall, Terrington St Clement, a late fifteenth century house with a much older pedigree. Sir Thomas Lovell held high office under the first two Tudors.

KING JOHN

Shortly before King John died at Newark (from eating too many lampreys it is said), he visited King's Lynn in an attempt to rally forces against the barons and the French. His return journey to Lincolnshire took him through Terrington St Clement and via Walpole Cross Keys. The king's route was a slightly longer and safer one, but he instructed that his slower baggage and treasure wagons should take the shorter route. On that October night in 1216 the wagons probably crossed the estuary of the then 'Welle Stream'. It is possible that in crossing on some causeway a huge tide or river bore overtook them, sweeping away the baggage and treasure. Everyone loves a mystery, and over the centuries numerous attempts have been made to locate King John's Treasure, the last in the vicinity of Walpole St Andrew. But The Wash still retains this secret.

THINGS TO DO

❶ African Violet Centre, Terrington St Clement (01553 828374) is a must for keen gardeners. It is situated beside the A17, five miles from King's Lynn and three miles from the A47/A17 junction .

❷ 'Peter Scott Walk': this was named in tribute to Sir Peter (1909-1989) for his work as a naturalist. Although just out of Norfolk, the East Lighthouse at the mouth of the River Nene, where he lived and worked, can be seen on this walk. This is not a circular walk but simply follows the top of the outer sea defence bank between West Lynn in Norfolk and the East Bank Picnic Place near Sutton Bridge in Lincolnshire. The Lincolnshire section may also be used by horse riders. The West Lynn starting point is close to the river ferry linking West Lynn with the main town. A rough track leads to the sea bank. The total walk is about ten miles, but it can be accessed (shortened) from a point called Ongar Hill, north of Terrington St Clement, approximately four miles from the West Lynn starting point. There is a small car park at Ongar Hill. Copies of the walk are available from the King's Lynn Tourist Information Centre (TIC) (01553 763044), as are ferry times for West Lynn.

❸ Terrington St Clement Church will interest 'church crawlers'. It is one of the longest churches in Norfolk, with a fine roof and font cover, and a First World War tribute window that includes the Serbian coat of arms and the stars and stripes. The church dates mostly from the 15th century, probably the third building here, the earliest most likely Saxon. It is built of Barnack stone from Northamptonshire. Part of Dorothy L Sayers 'Nine Tailors' was based on Terrington.

❹ 'Worth a Detour': a little inland is another fine church at Tilney All Saints, Norman in origin, with a massive landmark tower and spire. The nave has a beautiful hammerbeam roof from the 15th century, the same age as the stalls and misericords, and the main font is Elizabethan.

❺ Pubs: King William in Terrington St Clement (01553 828514). The Woolpack, Walpole Cross Keys (01553 828327).

The magnificent, painted font-cover in Terrington St. Clement church, is early 17th century. The paintings are thought to be Flemish.

2 – King's Lynn

*For some time past, I have taken a walk in the fields near Lynn of about an hour every morning before breakfast –
I have never yet got out before six, and never after seven. The fields are, in my eyes, particularly charming at that
time in the morning – the sun is warm and not sultry – and there is scarce a soul to be seen.*
(Fanny Burney, *Early Diary*)

King's Lynn's maritime history is part of the very fabric of the town; salt is in its pores. Walking the streets of the Old Town, the layers of history peel back for those with eyes to see. Walk along King Street or Nelson Street with their elegant Georgian houses. More accurately, we are seeing medieval bones with a Georgian skin, as at Hampton Court. The best craftsmen's skills were used – one of the tangible rewards for prosperous sea-captains. Pop in and out of the maze of narrow alleyways and courtyards. Look out for the late-medieval shop-front in King Street (nos. 28–32) itself concealing one of Lynn's oldest stone houses, dating back to the 12th century. The sea and its influence on Lynn is never far away. And of course that link is seen very clearly in the elegant 17th century Customs House, the building that has come to represent King's Lynn. It was built in 1683-5 by a local architect Henry Bell, (the 'Duke's Head' was also his design) and it has a fine lantern tower. It was used initially as a merchant exchange before becoming a Customs House. Today it houses the TIC, with an exhibition upstairs that tells the story of its former use, when George Vancouver's father was Deputy Collector of Customs. Just round the corner in King's Staithe Square look for the fine building called Bank House.

George Vancouver stands appropriately in front of the Customs House where his father was Deputy Collector of Customs.

GEORGE VANCOUVER (1757-1798)

In 1772 the 14-year-old George Vancouver (the surname is Dutch in origin) joined Captain Cook's 'Resolution'. Dr Burney, the local organist of St Margaret's Church, was also a friend of Cook. This or a Walpole family connection may have led to an introduction for the young boy. After accompanying Cook on two voyages, George Vancouver made his own considerable mark by exploring and charting the west coast of North America, after first mapping parts of Australia and New Zealand. He gave his name of course to Canada's lovely island and city.

The Red Mount Chapel dates from the 15h century and was a stopping place for pilgrims journeying to the shrine at Walsingham.

A second strand to its history is Lynn's prominence as a religious centre. For example, the Grey Friars, Black, Austin and White Friars all had houses here. Greyfriars Tower remained as a lookout tower. Lynn boasts three magnificent churches, All Saints', St Margaret's and St Nicholas'. Another of the town's remarkable religious buildings is the Red Mount Chapel (1485), an octagonal building on its own mound situated in a park area called 'The Walks'. A chapel inside has been described as a 'perfect miniature'. It dates from the early 16th century and served as a 'wayside chapel' for pilgrims journeying to Walsingham, England's premier medieval shrine. Another interesting ecclesiastical building is Thoresby College (1500-10) built to house 13 priests to act as chaplains to the Trinity Guild (see p.20).

In the earliest days, Lynn (Lena, Lenne, Lindo and Lun are possible early variants) was a small town confined within the seabank of the middle of three islands, the southern of which was occupied a little later by the White Friars.

There are later 17th and 18th frontages on earlier buildings, as at Thoresby College, Tudor in origin. Look out for the fine doorway on the left, with its rare parchment-fold panelling.

The magnificent twin towers of the west-front of St Margaret's (most unusual for a parish church) dating back to the 12th century. The nearer tower has a rare tide clock, showing high tides and the phases of the moon.

An ominous reminder of the vulnerability of King's Lynn, is this record of flood levels.

The south gate to the town of Lynn, the only remaining gateway, dates from the the mid-14th century and was rebuilt 100 years later. A London mason, Richard Harbanger, built it and it originally had a portcullis.

Soon after the Norman Conquest, Bishop Losinga, first bishop of Norwich, founded a Benedictine priory here (see Priory Lane), and commissioned St Margaret's Church, an enormous building of white limestone. In earlier days St Margaret's had a spire at the crossing. Look out for the interesting 17th century 'tide clock' at the west end. This would have given Lynn's mariners a tide reference. Inside the church are two of the finest brasses in England, to Robert Braunche and wives, and to Adam De Walsoken and wife. With its position close to the North Sea, Lynn became an important outlet for East Anglia's wool, salt and grain, and a centre for the import of Gascony wine, Baltic timber and Tyneside coal. By the 12th century it had become the principal east coast port between the Thames and the Humber and a little later it could claim to be the 4th port in the country.

King John gave Lynn its first 'Great Charter' in 1204 making it a 'free borough'. Bishop Turbus, third bishop of Norwich, took a great interest in the town and possibly under him it became 'Bishop's Lynn'. It was the Bishop who extended the town northwards across the Purfleet, in the 1140s, to take in newly-drained lands. This new development was given its own 'Tuesday Market Place' (see p.20) and its own Chapel of St Nicholas (1146), a daughter church, or Chapel of Ease of St Margaret's. Nothing of the Norman original remains. Its present lead-covered spire was designed by Sir George Gilbert Scott in 1871. King's Lynn was thus in effect two medieval towns: the first was between the Millfleet in the south and the Purfleet in the North, and the second was built on newly-reclaimed land between the Purfleet and the Fisherfleet. The later Customs House is on the boundary between the two. 'Fleet' is the name given to Lynn's inland waterways which were unfortunately largely responsible for the town's health problems as late as the 19th century. At least Victorian citizens could drown their sorrows, with an estimated 180 pubs in 1892, and quite understandably, five temperance societies!

MARGERY KEMPE (C1373-C1440)

Margery Kempe was the daughter of John of Brunham, five times mayor of Lynn. Margery married a Lynn burgess named John Kempe, and by him had fourteen children. After her conversion to Christianity, she travelled widely on pilgrimages, including Canterbury, Compostella, Jerusalem and Rome. It is said that her hysterical weeping and wailing during these journeys tended to annoy her fellow pilgrims, not surprisingly! She is credited with 'writing' the first English autobiography (1432-1436) – dictated to a local friar.

Autumn colours in the churchyard of this fine Chapel of St Nicholas.

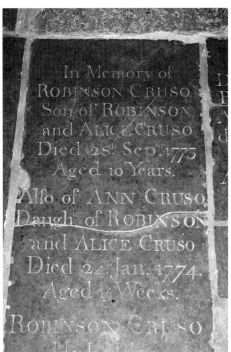

In Memory of
ROBINSON CRUSO
Son of ROBINSON
and ALICE CRUSO
Died 28ᵗʰ Sepʳ 1773
Aged 10 Years.

Also of ANN CRUSO
Daughᵗ of ROBINSON
and ALICE CRUSO
Died 22 Jan. 1774
Aged 16 Weeks.

ROBINSON CRUSO

It is said that Daniel Defoe saw this tomb-stone and used the name (slightly amended) for his hero, Robinson Crusoe.

Squares of black, knapped flint, local to Norfolk, with 'imported' limestone, create a spectacular, chequerboard pattern on the front of the Guildhall of the Holy Trinity.

It was the development of flourishing trade guilds (there were at least 75 guilds at various times) and also the Hanseatic League that made a major impact on the town's position and influence. Two fine guildhalls exist as a witness to the guilds' former importance. The Guildhall of the Holy Trinity, with its magnificent flint and limestone chequer-work, is in the Saturday Market Place. The town hall addition is Victorian but in the same style. It was in the Guildhall of St George (built 1406) in King Street that the Lord Admiral's Men, a company that included Shakespeare for a time, may have performed and Shakespeare possibly took part. Today the guildhall is a flourishing arts centre.

It was Henry VIII who transformed 'Bishop's Lynn' into 'King's Lynn' (1536) and by another charter (1537) granted its annual Mart, or Fair, in February and confirmed the two weekly markets. The Tuesday Market Place must surely be one of the most elegant market squares in the country, stretching to three acres in the heart of the town. Over the years it has been Lynn's traditional site for celebrations (as well as executions and witch-burnings). Its great fair starts on St Valentine's Day and lasts for a fortnight. As in many towns there would have been summary justice dispensed at the Court of 'Pie Powder' (pied poudre, or 'dusty feet') on every day of the fair.

Criminals also gathered here: in 1565 for example, the Sheriff of Norfolk, William Paston, was warned of such a company, 'a great brotherhood of them who be cut–purses and notable thieves that are appointed to meet at Lynn Mart'. 'The Guardians of the Peace', often a little elderly, and wearing tri-corn hats and hob-nailed boots, were known as Red Coats or 'Javelin Men'.

HANSEATIC LEAGUE

The Hansa was a late medieval federation of some 150 German towns and cities which dominated trade from the Atlantic to the Baltic and which even fought wars against its neighbours. The power of the league in England led to privileges not enjoyed by native merchants. The large 15th century Stafel Hof or 'Steelyard' can still be seen in St Margaret's Lane, where Norfolk wool was weighed before export, and casks of imported wine were stored. The league was dissolved in the 17th century. In recent years the Hanseatic League (HANSA) has been re-instated, and in 2005 King's Lynn had the honour of being elected to it as the first UK town.

Above: *Kings Lynn's St Valentine's Fair with the popular 'gallopers'. This roundabout is a Savage original, dating from 1895.*

Below: *Early morning sunshine for Kings Lynn's Tuesday market, against the splendid backdrop of the 17th century Duke's Head Hotel. It was designed by Henry Bell in 1684 and named after the Duke of York.*

FREDERICK SAVAGE
(1828–1897)

Frederick Savage was a remarkable man. His background was in engineering, and when he settled in Lynn in 1851 it was as a maker of agricultural machinery. He obviously gained a great deal more fun out of repairing and inventing fairground galloping horses, although his previous traction engines provided a useful background to this new challenge. The two strands of his work continued hand in hand, but as well as this he entered local politics, becoming an Alderman and then Mayor of Lynn.

Mayor Frederick Savage, fairground engineer extraordinary.

The 'Fisher Fleet' is the name of the waterway.

During the Civil War, the town lived up to its name and, exceptionally for East Anglia, declared its allegiance to the king. Parliament was disturbed and a detachment of troops under one Captain William Poe was despatched from Essex to cut the town off. The Earl of Manchester quickly followed, and at its height 8,000 troops were employed in the siege. A bombardment of the town started, with mortars set up on the Western side facing the town's quayside. On a September Sunday in 1643 an 18lb shot landed in St Margaret's, in the middle of a service. A cannon ball can be seen in the entrance porch to Hampton Court! When there was no royal reassurance from the king, support ebbed. Manchester told the leaders of the besieged town to remove their women and children before the final bloody onslaught, and named the day. It was too much, and Sir Hamon le Strange, the Governor, opened negotiations for a surrender.

Fishing in all its forms remained a large part of Lynn's lifeblood, with its fishing fleet chasing everything from shrimps to whales, with whitefish and shellfish in between. From the early 17th century to the early 19th, it gained importance from its association with the Greenland Whaling Fishery, and 'blubber houses' with their terrible stench were to be found along the quayside, extracting oil for use in lighting. The advent of gas during the first half of the 19th century destroyed the trade. The 'Greenland Fishery' in Bridge Street is a reminder, and was once an alehouse for Greenland sailors. Between 1867-9 a large new dock complex was built, called the Alexander Dock, catering for the large ships that have increasingly used the port, and the Bentinck Dock was built shortly afterwards, in 1883. Over the last century or so further additions have been made to cater for shipping's technological developments. The riverside quay (1992) caters for much larger vessels.

King's Lynn is facing the challenges of the present century in the way it has faced those of previous centuries, and large regeneration projects are in preparation or planning. One such is the Nar Ouse Regeneration Area (NORA), creating a large new community on derelict land, with a marina as a later stage proposal.

FANNY BURNEY (1752-1840)

In 1751 Charles Burney was appointed as organist of St Margaret's Church, and the following year his daughter Fanny was born. She lived in Lynn until the family moved to London eight years later. Her first novel 'Evelina', was published (anonymously) in 1778 and became a great success. It earned her £20 it is said. 'Cecilia' followed in 1782. During this period she got to know Dr Johnson well. Her prominence led to a royal appointment, that of 'Second Keeper of the Robes' to Queen Charlotte, in 1786. She resigned however five years later, with a gold watch and a pension of £100 per annum. In 1793 she married General Alexandre d'Arblay and lived in France for several years. In 1815 they returned to England, and after her husband's death she worked on literary tasks for the rest of her life. Her brother James Burney (1750—1821), later Rear Admiral, sailed with Vancouver on Cook's voyages.

1 **Customs House**, Purfleet Quay (01553 763044). On the floor above the TIC, are displays featuring the merchants, customs men and smugglers of Lynn.

2 **Ferry from King's Lynn-West Lynn:** a ferry has existed here since 1285! It runs each weekday, at twenty-minute intervals, but can obviously be suspended if weather conditions would make the crossing dangerous.

3 **Green Quay (The Wash Discovery Centre)**, South Quay (01553 818500). Situated in a 16th century warehouse, the centre is dedicated to The Wash and its wildlife.

4 **Lynn Museum**, Old Market Street (01553 775001). This museum tells the story of King's Lynn (re-opens Spring 2006).

5 **St Nicholas Chapel** is worth a visit (key from the Tudor Rose Hotel). Find the tombstone to Robinson Cruso, believed to have given Daniel Defoe the name for his hero. Lookout also for the large ship's anchor.

6 **Tales of the Old Gaol House**, Saturday Market Place (01553 774297). Meet local criminals from the past. This museum also includes Lynn's civic treasures.

7 **Town House Museum of Lynn Life**, 46, Queen St (01553 773450). Reconstructed rooms through the ages show everyday life in Lynn.

8 **True's Yard, Fishing Heritage Museum**, North Street (01553 770479): an independent museum telling the story of Lynn's maritime past. It is housed in two former fishermen's cottages. It also offers research facilities for genealogy.

9 **Walks:** well worth buying from the TIC for a few pence, even for the drawings alone, are the following 'history trail' leaflets: 'King's Lynn Maritime Trail' and 'King's Lynn Town Walk'. Also good value as souvenirs are the coloured fact-sheets on the two market places, and on the Purfleet.

10 **Pubs and eating places:** Duke's Head hotel, built 17th century (01553 774996); Lattice House, 16th century timbered building (01553 769585); Tudor Rose hotel, St Nicholas Street, (01553 762824) is reputed to be the oldest building for a pub in Lynn, dating back to 1187. It was possibly part of the winter palace of a Norfolk bishop; Crofters and Riverside Restaurant at the King's Lynn Arts Centre, King Street; Rembrandt's, Chapel Street. Many more.

11 **Concerts and drama** at King's Lynn Arts Centre and the Corn Exchange.

12 **'Coasthopper'** bus service (King's Lynn to Sheringham with Cromer connections and through tickets), provides flexible support in planning walks.

13 **'Worth a look':** the amazing Carnegie Library building in London Road.

14 **Film:** watch the film 'Revolution': King's Lynn as 18th century New York.

True's Yard Museum dedicated to the history of the 'North End' the former fishermen's quarter.

3 – Castle Rising, Wolferton and Sandringham

Rising was a sea-port town, when Lynn was but a marsh, now Lynn is a sea-port town,
and Rising fears the worse.
(old saying).

About 5 miles north of King's Lynn if you turn left off the A149, Queen Elizabeth Way, you come to the quiet village of Castle Rising. This was once a bustling port at the mouth of the River Babingley. The market cross is still on the green by the church and the port was situated to the north-west; by the 15th century the ships had become too large and the port was becoming less accessible because of its silting up. It was a 'rotten borough' and up to 1832 returned two members of parliament.

The main feature of the village is the castle. It stands at the eastern edge, within great earthworks, the whole site covering about 12 acres. It was built by one William d'Albini to celebrate his marriage to the widow of Henry I and the acquisition of the earldom of Sussex. Its most famous resident was Queen Isabella, wife of Edward II. Isabella was sent there in 1331 by her son, Edward III, after she had been found guilty of her husband's murder, along with her lover Mortimer. Mortimer was not so lucky and was put to death. Isabella was not a prisoner at Castle Rising - she was able to come and go as she pleased. She had a pension of £3,000 per year and remained here, along with her retinue and household of 180 people, for 30 years. The castle remained the property of the Crown until the 16th century and the site is now administered by English Heritage.

The church of St Lawrence, though greatly restored, contains many Norman or Romanesque features. These can be found on the west front and in the interior of the church. The Norman font came from an older church near the castle, and as it is carved only on two sides it is thought to have stood in a corner there. The church was dedicated to St Felix who brought Christianity to East Anglia. In visiting this area he landed at nearby Babingley.

To the east of the church is a group of Jacobean Almshouses known as The Hospital of the Holy and Undivided Trinity. The village of Castle Rising today may well belie its former importance, but its history rings out from its very stones. It is very well worth exploring and will reward the visitor who decides to take this small detour.

The Market Cross, illustrating the past importance of Castle Rising, stands close to the site of the old port.

William d'Albini's fortress built in 1140.

The Hospital of the Holy and Undivided Trinity.

The 'grave and discreet' ladies of Trinity Hospital.

The early Norman font in St Lawrence's church has three cats' faces, possibly a humorous reference by the mason to the fact that Felix (to whom the old church was dedicated) is Latin for 'cat'.

THE HOSPITAL OF THE HOLY AND UNDIVIDED TRINITY

Trinity Hospital was built in 1609–15 at a cost of £451 by Henry Howard, Earl of Northampton, who was a younger brother of the Duke of Norfolk. 'Hospitals' in earlier days had a slightly different role. They were set up as houses of charity for the old and infirm, rather than simply for the sick. In his will, Henry Howard stated 'that myne heir shall have the placinge and displacinge… of the pore of the Hospitall of Rising.' Rising Hospital was founded for women, and according to the statutes 'they must be of honest life and conversation, religious, grave and discreet… to be fifty six years of age at least and no common beggar, harlot, scold or drunkard...' On Sundays and on special occasions such as Founder's Day the pensioners wear bright red cloaks bearing the Howard Arms. The tall, black conical hats are worn just on these special occasions. At other times a more modern hat is worn. The Matron of the Hospital wears a hat of a different style. The Jacobean building is made from local red brick and is now governed by the Mercers' Company of London with a board of local trustees.

This station lamp echoes its past royal connections.

This interesting 'royal' signal box takes our eye along the former track-bed towards Wolferton Church.

Just north of Castle Rising is the village of Wolferton. The name means 'the town or settlement of a man called Wulfere.' Despite its early origin there is no mention of Wolferton in the Domesday Book. Its main claim to fame in more recent times has been its connection with royalty.

In 1862 a house at Sandringham was purchased by Queen Victoria and Prince Albert for the Prince of Wales, the future King Edward VII, and it was he who extended it. Initially the royal train would terminate its journey at King's Lynn, but with the opening of the branch line to Hunstanton, a royal station was built at Wolferton. The line has long since been closed but for years afterwards the station was a popular museum with a large collection of royal memorabilia and a magnificent royal 'loo'!

Today the station buildings are little changed from their railway days. Even though they are now private houses the railway atmosphere is still present. If you look around you will see the former glory in the lamps and the clock tower. On the opposite side of the road is the old signal box, again in private hands. Look beyond the signal box and you will see the church and beyond that the marshes bordering the Great Ouse estuary and The Wash.

Sandringham House is the private residence of Her Majesty Queen Elizabeth II. It is not a royal palace belonging to the state but the private retreat of the monarchy and has been since Edward became king in 1901. There is no village of Sandringham and there never has been. The name is derived from the house and its estate. It does, however, have a parish church serving the royal family, their staff and tenants. The Queen and other members of the Royal Family regularly spend Christmas and New Year at Sandringham, and use it at other times of the year when visiting Norfolk. When they are not in residence the house and grounds are at times open to the public. The church is also a 'must' for visitors to Sandringham. The pulpit is built of oak and panelled in solid silver. The silver altar and reredos were presented by Rodman Wannamaker in memory of Edward VII.

Sandringham House, Norfolk's royal retreat, from across the lake.

The Wolferton village sign depicts the Norse legend of Tyr, a villager and Fenrir, an evil wolf who had been terrorising the villagers. Woden sent a slender, miraculous cord to assist the village. Tyr challenged Fenrir to a contest of strength using the cord. Fenrir agreed only on the condition that Tyr put his right arm in the wolf's mouth. The outcome of the contest was that Fenrir was shackled, but Tyr lost his arm!

The Sandringham Estate extends to the Wash and over many years has taken part in reclamation projects. The estate is mainly farmed or forested, and is run commercially by the Land Agent on the Queen's behalf. Apart from the house itself, here are also two studs, a fruit farm, extensive gardens, a museum and a country park. Access to the country park is freely available all year. The latter comprises carefully managed woodland and heath, with nature trails and camping and caravan club sites. There is also a Visitor Centre with a gift shop and restaurant. The estate hosts craft fairs and country shows from time to time, culminating in the ever popular Sandringham Flower Show, held each July, where you can 'rub shoulders' with royalty.

THINGS TO DO

❶ **Castle Rising Castle** (01553 631330): extensive ruins of medieval castle with fine keep.

❷ **The Hospital of the Trinity Guild**, (01553 631270): 17th century almshouses, regularly open. Telephone for details.

❸ **Sandringham House** (01553 612908): something for everyone: visit the house, museum and gardens.

❹ **Churches:** St Lawrence, Castle Rising: Norman church with many interesting Romanesque features; St Mary Magdalene, Sandringham: original medieval church with splendid royal treasures and memorials, re-built in the sixteenth century.

❺ **Walks:** Castle Rising to Roydon Common and return: an 8 mile circular walk on lanes and old railway track. Start near the castle; Sandringham Park: woodland walk in the garden; two nature trails, (1 mile and 2 miles) but also many other paths.

❻ **Pubs and eating places:** The Black Horse, (01553 631225), The Post Office Tea Rooms, (01553 631211) both in Castle Rising; Visitor Centre Restaurant, Sandringham House (01553 612908).

❼ **'Worth a detour':** Houghton Hall (01485 528569), off A148 : the home of Britain's first Prime Minister, Sir Robert Walpole.

4 – Dersingham, Snettisham and Heacham

On summer evenings, we often on a Sunday would take a walk. This would involve… whoever in the family… happened to be living with or visiting Grandfather at the time. One of the favourite walks we had was across the common and the Princess' Drive… it started at the top of Sandringham Hill… until it exited at the Wolferton Road… there were excellent views across the fens and marshes to the distant Wash.
(Harry Thorpe, *Recollections of Dersingham Life.*)

The village of Dersingham grew up because it was near the sea but on sufficiently high ground to avoid flooding; it was also on a line of springs so there was plenty of fresh water. The village was founded in ancient times by a chief named Derosige. 'Ham' means 'village' so today's name is a corruption of 'Derosige's village'.

The older houses in the village are constructed mainly of carstone or flint. The carstone, quarried in the area, is a type of sandstone known locally as 'gingerbread stone'. The church of St Nicholas is built of this stone but has limestone dressings. The chancel and nave date from the early 14th century whilst the tower is late 15th century. The Tithe Barn, near the church, was built in 1671 of carstone and clunch, a form of chalk, with brick dressings. It was never used for tithes and now belongs to the Sandringham Estate who lease it to Norfolk County Council. Dersingham Hall, originally constructed in the 16th century, was converted into a hotel in the 1980s. Over 100 years ago Dersingham was a sizeable village with a population of over 1,000 people. With the coming of the railway this grew and the current population is nearly 5,000.

West Norfolk's local building stone is called carstone.

Dersingham Bog is a National Nature Reserve and is on the royal estate close to the A149. It is managed by English Nature and has three distinct habitats, mire, heath and woodland. The mire includes plants such as bog asphodel, bog moss and round-leaved sundew. A steep escarpment on one side marks the ancient coastline and here the heath and woodland are found. Birds that can be seen here include redpoll, crossbill, long-eared owl and sparrowhawk. Two car parks provide easy access. The station was a typical rural one with facilities for passengers and for the farming community. Farm products went out and coal, fresh food and other domestic products came in. Dersingham was at the half-way point on the old Lynn to Hunstanton line. This line was completed in 1862 having taken just 15 months to build and it closed in 1969.

A fine 17th century barn built largely of carstone.

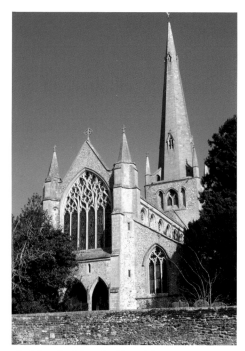

St Mary's Church, Snettisham.

CARSTONE

Carstone is a type of sandstone which is rich in iron oxide. Under this name it is found mainly in the east of England. Its general name is Lower Greensand. It is coarse, pebbly and gritty and is always some shade of brown, ranging from café au lait to deep chocolate in colour. Norfolk people often call it 'gingerbread' stone. It is rather soft when quarried but becomes harder on exposure to the air. It is not good enough for carving.

The village of Snettisham has many buildings built of the local carstone (see below). It has a gently shelving beach of sand and shingle, two miles in length with fine views over The Wash.

There is an RSPB reserve here where you can see a huge variety of waders, and large numbers of common terns and black-headed gulls nest here in the summer. The reserve is the place to witness two of the UK's wildlife spectacles: at high tide, more especially so at an exceptional high tide, tens of thousands of wading birds are pushed off their feeding grounds on to the roosting grounds in front of the hides. Spectacle number two takes place in mid-winter, either at dawn or dusk, when flights of thousands of pink-footed geese fly between their safe roosting site on The Wash and the farmland where they feed on the remains of the sugar beet harvest. The RSPB produces information on the best times to see these birds.

The cruciform church of St Mary stands in an imposing position on higher ground at the edge of the village. It is one of a few Norfolk churches to have a spire. At first it appears to have the tower at the eastern end of the church but on closer inspection the present building finishes at what was once the crossing, so the tower was originally a central tower. The now non-existent chancel extended for 40 feet beyond the present east wall. At the west end, the church has a rare Galilee Porch. It has a groined roof with a small room above. Another interesting feature is the Saunce or Sanctus Bell which is probably 13th century, thus making it one of the oldest bells in the country.

Snettisham's claim to fame is the discovery of the richest Iron Age treasure ever found in this country. The first discovery was made in 1948 when a field was being ploughed deeper than usual. The ploughman discovered an interesting lump of metal. He showed it to his foreman who decided it was a piece from an old brass bedstead and threw it to the side of the field. During the next few days however, more pieces of metal turned up and a local businessman recognised their age and took them to Norwich Castle Museum where their importance was confirmed. So the 'brass bedstead' was recognised as being a gold torque. A torque was worn around the neck and was the Celtic equivalent of the coronet worn during the Middle Ages. This led to further excavations and in all some 30 kg of treasure were found, including bracelets, torques and coins, much of it gold and silver. The latest were found in the 1990s. The treasure can be seen in Norwich Castle Museum and the British Museum.

At the time of the Domesday Book there were seven mills in Snettisham, more than in any other village in Norfolk. There is still a water-mill today and its origins are unique. It was built, possibly on the site of a former mill, in 1800 'by the people for the people'. The poorer members of the parish were able to bring any corn they had grown, or had gleaned, to be milled. It is built of carstone quarried in Snettisham.

Heacham is at the heart of the Norfolk lavender industry. The first settlers came here as early as 3,000 BC but little is known until the 11th century when the village took its name from one Geoffrey de Hechem. In the 17th century, the local squire John Rolfe, surprisingly married an American Indian princess called Pocahontas (see p.36). The church of St Mary dates from the late 13th century and is Early English. Originally cruciform in design it has changed much over the years. A bell, predating the church, hangs in a cupola on the tower and is dated at about 1100 which makes it the oldest bell in East Anglia and the seventh oldest in the country. Heacham's two fine beaches with views across The Wash are its attractions today together with the glorious scent of lavender!

NORFOLK LAVENDER

In 1932 a local Norfolk nurseryman planted six acres of lavender and from this grew the industry which exists today. Now there are over 100 acres containing hedgerows of lavender bushes. Pure lavender oil is still distilled from the original secret recipe. The industry is based at Caley Mill and today produces some 23 different products. The range includes everything from the original Lavender Cologne to bottles of oils or lotions made from other scented plants such as Lily of the Valley. In 1997 a four acre Scented Garden was opened which is appreciated by the visually impaired.

Sea bindweed is a low growing gem of the dunes, much more attractive than its hedgerow cousin.

Caley Mill, the home of Norfolk lavender.

The work of sea defence is never ending. Here at Heacham's North Beach, bulldozers are strengthening the bank.

With its bright orange–red legs, the redshank is a distinctive and noisy bird. It probes the mud of estuaries and coastal flatlands, and nests in marshes, and meadows.

The male shelduck has a coral-pink bill with a knob at the base. Shelduck pair up for more than one season. It is the largest duck in the British Isles, feeding on muddy estuaries and shorelines.

POCAHONTAS

Pocahontas was born in 1595/6 at Chesapeake Bay, Virginia, the daughter of Chief Powhatan, the chief of some 40 Algonquin Indian villages. The English settled in this area under the leadership of Captain John Smith. There were various skirmishes with the Indians and on one occasion Smith was captured and about to be put to death when Pocahontas intervened and saved his life. The settlement grew under the name of Jamestown, and Smith, having been injured in a gunpowder explosion, returned to England. Pocahontas married one of the tribe but he died within three years. John Rolfe of Heacham and his English wife arrived at Jamestown where John was trading in tobacco. His wife died soon after their arrival and John fell in love with Pocahontas. They married, and with their young son Thomas, returned to England in 1616. She was the subject of much curiosity and was presented at court and at other gatherings of the nobility. In 1617 the Rolfes prepared to leave England and return to Virginia. Pocahontas became ill, possibly with tuberculosis, and was put ashore at Gravesend where she died. It is thought she is buried in a vault beneath the chancel in Gravesend parish church. During her stay in England she possibly stayed at Heacham Hall.

One of England's most unusual village signs, showing Pocahontas, a Native American princess.

THINGS TO DO

❶ **Churches to visit:** St Nicholas, Dersingham; St Mary the Virgin, Snettisham; St Mary the Virgin, Heacham.

❷ **Dersingham Bog:** (01733 455101). This is a national nature reserve on the line of the ancient coast managed by English Nature.

❸ **Norfolk Lavender:** (01485 570384), Caley Mill, Heacham. The home of English lavender; visit the herb garden and collection of lavender species growing near Caley Mill or try the lavender flavoured scones in the restaurant.

❹ **RSPB Snettisham Reserve:** (01485 542689). Summer or winter bird lovers or non-ornithologists will find something of interest in this popular reserve.

❺ **Walks:** Dersingham Bog, (01733 455101); circular walk of 1.5 miles, part-suited for wheelchairs; A circular walk from Snettisham to Shernborne and Sedgeford; this interesting 11 mile walk starts at Snettisham church; an easy 4.5 mile return walk from Snettisham to Ingoldisthorpe

❻ **Pubs and eating places:** Feathers Hotel, (01485 540207), frequented by Edward VII as Prince of Wales, and The Coach and Horses, (01485 540391) both in Dersingham; The Rose and Crown, (01485 541382), and The Queen Victoria (01485 541344) in Snettisham; Rushmore's Restaurant, (01485 579393), Fox & Hounds (01485 570345), The Wheatsheaf (01485 570282), The West Norfolk, (01485 570348), all in Heacham.

Hunstanton to Holkham

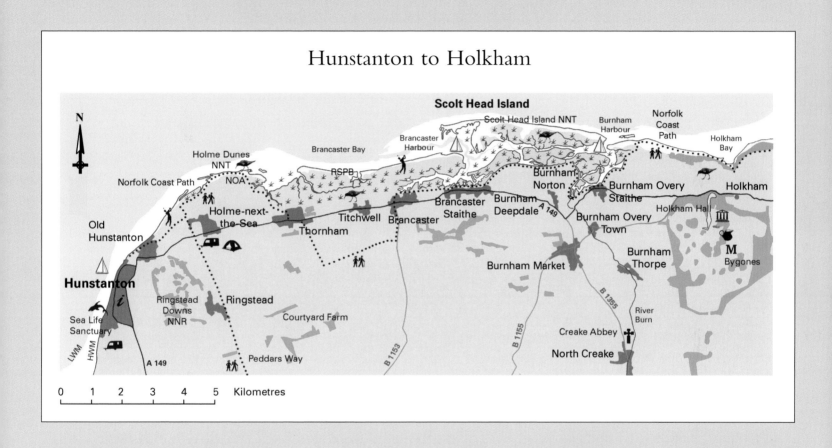

A nautical skeleton lies underneath Hunstanton's unique cliff strata. St Edmund's Point is 60 feet high.

5 – Hunstanton

I spent most of my time on the moat, which is really a sizeable lake. I'm writing this in the punt with my typewriter on a bed-table wobbling on one of the seats. There is a duck close by which utters occasional quacks that sound like a man with an unpleasant voice saying nasty things in an undertone.
(P.G. Wodehouse at Hunstanton Hall)

Hunstanton ('Hunston' to some) is in reality Norfolk's first 'New Town', conceived and brought to fruition by the local squire assisted by the Great Eastern Railway. The history of Hunstanton (both parts) and the Le Strange family have been inextricably linked for nine centuries or more. For 'Hunstanton' in the historical sense read 'Old Hunstanton' and for the Hunstanton of holiday-makers and day-trippers read 'Hunstanton St Edmunds', a town created where open fields had been before. It was a town planned by Henry Styleman le Strange, probably on his stroll across the estate in the company of his friend Charles Bagot, heading for the sea and an early morning dip. His idea was for a coastal holiday village with a triangular green sloping down to the sea and a prospectus was issued in 1845. The first 'house' built here the following year was somewhat sensibly the New Inn, later 'The Golden Lion'. It was known predictably as 'le Strange's Folly' but offered good Norfolk beer at 1d a pint and stabling at 6d. It is still in the heart of the town.

Hunstanton's town sign shows its link with St Edmund. It shows the wolf that guarded the saint's head after his execution and the sun setting over the sea.

Unfortunately subsequent development was a little slow until the Great Eastern decided to build a branch line from King's Lynn to Hunstanton in 1862. The line was engineered by John Sutherland Valentine at a cost of £80,000. Ironically it was the year Le Strange died. When the railway was at its height it also served to transport tons of cockles. In 1912 there was a serious accident here when the London train failed to stop, and ended up against the billiard room of the (GER's own) Sandringham Hotel. Luckily no-one was killed. The railway closed in 1969.

In its Victorian and Edwardian heyday there would be horse-drawn wagonettes parked ready to take visitors on excursions, perhaps to Ringstead Downs. Motor coaches of course followed. The resort became a popular destination, even for members of the Royal Family at nearby Sandringham. In 1873 a town guide could claim: 'The New

The Golden Lion Hotel (formerly the New Inn) was the first building in 'New ' Hunstanton. Beyond is the Town Hall.

Beach huts sheltering in the dunes at Old Hunstanton

Town of St Edmunds is in the vicinity of the railway station, handsome and substantially built'. Because the local squire had had the idea for the new town on an open site, and still retained control of what happened here, it was possible at the beginning to create a unified architectural style, sometimes with turrets more reminiscent of a French chateau and with the liberal use of the local carstone. New Hunstanton's development was therefore a measured one at the beginning but later, after the camps and caravan parks followed, its popularity soared. Some visitors were attracted by the area's curative spring waters.

'Hunstanton St Edmunds' was so called because the saint supposedly landed here in 855 on his return from Germany, to be crowned. The ruined chapel near the lighthouse was where pilgrims could say prayers before taking these healing waters. The chapel dates back to 1272. The present lighthouse was built in 1844 but the first one was as early as 1666. During the First World War it was used as a secret wireless and observation station, monitoring German naval movements and it closed down in 1921.

Hunstanton Hall: The porch with its shell design, dated 1618, survived the fire of 1853.

Above: *The chapel of St Edmund, dating from 1272, commemorates his landing here.*

Left: *Elegant carstone villas are a feature of Hunstanton's architecture.*

The area of Old Hunstanton had a much longer pedigree, stretching back at least to the Stone Age or early Bronze Age (1500-2000BC). The pre-Roman Icknield Way finished here and the ancient Peddars Way crossed the present golf course to the ferry terminal that the Romans needed for quick transit to and from Lincolnshire. There is even a Roman bridge here.

The Anglo Saxons had settled here certainly by AD 500, and the first mention of the name was in the will of Bishop Aelfric of Elmham concerning land held under King Harold at 'Hunstanes-Tune'. There was a church in the old village at the time of Domesday, though the present church is mainly 14th century.

The le Strange family seat was at Hunstanton Hall, in the old village. The house is early 16th century in origin, but it suffered a terrible fire in April 1853, and was rebuilt. The fire engine having to come from Heacham. There was a building on an island in the lake for an earlier le Strange to practice his viol, so perhaps he played rather badly! A later visitor who also found the water beneficial to creativity was P.G.Wodehouse. He apparently visited often, and penned some of the 'Jeeves' stories in a punt on the moat. Like all good mansions Hunstanton Hall has a 'grey lady' – the ghost of Dame Armine le Strange.

There has been a lighthouse in Hunstanton since 1666.

Lowry-like figures populate Hunstanton's glittering sands.

A pier was built in 1870 as a facility for visitors to the town. It was 830 feet long and from 1890 boasted a theatre. An iron staircase led down to diving boards at different levels. There were live shows every weekend, such as the popular pierrots and it even had a miniature railway. The pier suffered a fire in 1939 that destroyed the pavilion, and it never fully recovered. In 1978 after serious storm damage it was finally demolished. Its moment of glory was the filming of 'Barnacle Bill' starring Alec Guiness (1957).

Hunstanton has a long lifeboat history, the first boat being based on the beach at 'Old Hunstanton' (originally a fishing village) and in 1867 the RNLI based a boat here. The turn-of-the-century boat-shed can still be visited, but the boat is now a high-tech fast response Atlantic class vessel. Hunstanton also has an RNLI hovercraft, one of the few stations around the coast to be given this very useful craft.

Fulmars have been in Norfolk since 1947 and are found wherever there are cliffs. They are true sea-birds, often following the fishing boats, gliding on wings over 1m wide.

From the outset there was something just a little bit 'special' about Hunstanton as a resort. For a start, it is the only major East Coast resort to face westwards. Then, where else would you find cliffs like the layers of ice cream in an old fashioned wafer? Hunstanton has them, providing interest for tourists and birds alike, and causing geologists to drool at the mouth. Technically it is Norfolk carstone with bands of white chalk and red chalk. Look out for the combination of these rocks in the cottage walls of Old Hunstanton. The cliffs are at their highest at St Edmund's Point, near the lighthouse, where they reach 60 feet. The chalk layers contain fossils such as ammonites, belemnites and brachiopods. In the early 20th century part of the cliff here contained a 'scooped out' hollow, that formed a natural amphitheatre for presentations, including children's shows.

Recently Hunstanton has become one of the leading UK destinations for water sports and in 2005 it was chosen to host the World Water Ski Racing Championships. Today, as in Victorian times, Hunstanton continues to offer something for everyone. It has large 'award-winning' sandy beaches with safe shallow water - and of course those legendary sunsets over The Wash.

Sunday morning 'spruce-up' at Hunstanton's lifeboat station, one of very few in the UK to be given a hovercraft in addition to its 'Atlantic 75'.

❶ Boat trips to Seal Island : Searles Seatours (01485 534444).

❷ Boston Square Sensory Park is a special area for the elderly and sensory-handicapped, created from a derelict square.

❸ Hunstanton Sea Life Sanctuary on the southern promenade (01485 533576) is an aquarium and leading marine rescue centre.

❹ Oasis Leisure Centre, central promenade (01485 534227) has a range of water attractions in a series of leisure pools, plus squash, racquet ball, bowls, table tennis and roller skating.

❺ Princess Theatre, The Green (01485 532252).

❻ St Mary's Church and the village of Old Hunstanton are worth a visit. In the graveyard are the (marked) graves of a soldier and a customs officer who met cruel deaths at the hands of smugglers.

❼ TIC, Town Hall, The Green (01485 532610).

The church of St Mary in Old Hunstanton.

❽ Walks: The Norfolk Coast Path (01328 711533) begins in Hunstanton, running through the 'Area of Outstanding Natural Beauty' and crossing the ancient Peddars Way at Holme. A shorter walk from the above, along the top of the cliffs will take you to the lighthouse and chapel, or a little further to the dunes of Old Hunstanton beach.

❾ Pubs and eating places: The Golden Lion, (01485 532688), was New Hunstanton's first building; the Le Strange Arms (Ancient Mariner Inn), (01485 534411) Old Hunstanton, The Neptune, (01485 532122) Old Hunstanton.

❿ 'Worth a detour': Ringstead Downs and Courtyard Farm, Ringstead (01485 525251) an organically-run farm with permitted walks, a farm shop and bunkhouse accommodation, (01485 525654). If you take this detour try 'The Gintrap Inn' (01485 525264) in Ringstead, an 18th century coaching inn.

Autumn sunshine on Old Hunstanton's dunes.

6 – Holme-next-the-Sea, Thornham and Titchwell

Here under lieth Richard Stone and Clemens his wife, who lived in wedlock joyfully together
64 years and three months; of them proceeded 7 sons and 6 daughters, & from those and their(s) issued
72 children, which the said Richard and Clemens to their great comfort did behold
(Richard Stone monument, 1607, St Mary's Church, Holme)

Holme-next-the-Sea was the end point of the Peddars Way, the ancient trackway that crosses Norfolk. The Iceni tribes lived in this area and built a series of small hill forts. Holme is a pretty village; note the variety of building materials used in the cottages and the church including clunch. The church was made smaller in the 18th century, for reasons of expensive maintenance.

In 1998 a series of posts emerged on the beach at Holme that gradually showed their shape as a circle. They were discovered by a local man, John Lorimer. The impact of the discovery of what became known as 'Seahenge' sent ripples around the world and brought to the fore a number of burning conservation issues. Not only was there considerable controversy as to whether the circle of posts should be moved from the original site to allow conservation of the timbers to take place, but the siting of the circle, so very close to major nature reserves, added complications. When 'Seahenge' featured in national newspapers and hundreds of people wanted to see it, serious worries were expressed about the disturbance to key plants and wildlife. Interestingly, the land between high and low water, the 'foreshore', is traditionally within the property of the Crown. In the case of Holme this was not so, as way back in the 13th century the local Le Strange family had been given this privilege, together with the title 'Lord High Admiral of the Wash' (a Gilbert and Sullivan ring about that). In fact their demesne extended 'as far as a man could ride on a white charger and throw a spear'. Where the spear landed was the extent of the Le Strange lands. Just how good their spear-throwing was, or how many white horses the family owned, is left to the mists of history!

Seahenge was built on a 'submerged forest' outcrop, and it may have had some connection with funerary rites. The thick peat layer had been responsible for its preservation. Having

A pair of avocets at Titchwell. This bird is the symbol of the RSPB. It has a slender upturned bill which it uses in shallow water, sweeping from side to side.

Shrubby seablite provides the first cover for migrant birds arriving across the North Sea.

The Bronze Age wooden circle, nicknamed 'Seahenge', created world-wide interest.

A lone figure walks the bank as the sun sets over Thornham.

46

been exposed, the time clock was ticking fast. Some still felt 'Seahenge' should be allowed to fade into the past again. After much debate, the Bronze Age timbers were taken to Flag Fen (Cambridgeshire), to be washed and examined. They were then taken to the Mary Rose site to be preserved prior to display in King's Lynn. Ironically, a second even larger circle subsequently emerged.

Holme Dunes Nature Reserve is so important that it is designated an SSSI, a 'National Nature Reserve', and a 'Wetland of International Importance'. It provides a unique habitat that attracts countless birds such as the sanderling, knot, grey plover and bar-tailed godwit. In spring and early summer the reserve becomes home to many other breeding colonies such as oystercatchers, little terns and ringed plovers. There is also a great variety of flowers and insects including marsh helleborines and grayling butterflies. There is also an important Norfolk Ornithologist's Association reserve at Holme.

A very high tide provides a delightful early morning scene, looking towards Thornham's coal barn.

Thornham was probably a Roman signal station for the ferry at Holme. In the Middle Ages it was a flourishing harbour, but all that remains today of its former importance is a solitary 'coal barn' a reminder of the pre-railway age, when colliers from the north of England regularly supplied our coasts with 'sea-coal'. Between 1887 and 1926, Thornham had a famous iron foundry, set up by the lady of the Manor, Mrs Ames Lydd. It commanded a world-wide reputation and was patronized by the royal family. It also won a gold medal at an international exhibition in Brussels. Thornham sign shows this foundry. Thornham's church has Norman origins. Look out for the interesting 15th century poppyheads.

Titchwell, mentioned in the Domesday Book, has a village cross beside the main road, used by travelling preachers and pilgrims to Walsingham. Do visit the delightful Norman church with its tiny spirelet. The RSPB reserve is their most visited site in the UK. From World War II defensive flooding of the area a remarkable development has taken place. It is now possible to explore a range of habitats such as shingle banks, tidal saltmarshes, freshwater marshes and wet grazing-meadows.

THE PEDDARS WAY

The Peddars Way was possibly a pre-Roman trackway running some 40 miles from Thetford to the coast near Brancaster. It has ancient earthworks scattered along its route. It was possibly some kind of trade route originally, but the Romans needed to move around their conquered territories quickly, and so it was reconstructed by them to serve their military purposes, the quick movement of troops to where they were needed. In medieval times it would have been used by pilgrims and also as a trade route, for commodities such as salt for example.

THINGS TO DO

❶ **Holme Dunes Nature Reserve** (01603 625540) is managed by the Norfolk Wildlife Trust.

❷ **Holme Bird Observatory** (01485 525406) is part of the Norfolk Ornithologists' Association.

❸ **Titchwell Reserve** (01485 210779) where you can explore the range of habitats such as shingle banks, tidal salt-marshes, fresh water marshes and wet grazing-meadows. It is signposted between Titchwell and Thornham.

❹ **Walks:** the Holme reserves can be reached from Thornham along a raised bank, starting just beyond the 'coal barn'. Alternatively take the road signposted NNT (now Norfolk Wildlife Trust) just west of Holme and choose to park (private car park/ refreshments in season) and walk to the reserves, or drive the unmade road to the NWT. The 1km walk to the beach from the Titchwell visitor centre (car-parking fee only for non-members) is well worth it even for non–ornithologists.

❺ **Pubs and eating places:** Lifeboat Inn, Thornham (01485 512236), a 16th century smuggling inn on the edge of the marshes, is very convenient for refreshments, and accommodation is available. The bar even has an ancient game called pennies, the aim of which is to flick old pennies against an upright metal plate and to land them in a hole in front; The King's Head, Thornham (01485 512213); Titchwell Manor, a Victorian house (01485 210221) and the White Horse in Holme (01485 525512).

For many years from his arrival in 1993, Titchwell's mascot was Sammy, the black-winged stilt. It was estimated that one million visitors had seen Sammy.

Left: *the Lifeboat Inn, Thornham, a sixteenth century former smugglers' ale house on the edge of the marshes.*

Right: *Magical reed beds are just one of Titchwell's diverse habitats.*

7 – Brancaster

Got up about six o'clock this morning and set off before breakfast for Brancaster, about five miles from Burnham.
Got there about eight o'clock, called there on Mr. Shute the Rector, found him a-bed but he soon came down, and I
breakfasted, dined, supped and slept at the Farm House where Mr. Shute boards, one Farmer Chadwick—a large farmer.
(Parson Woodforde's diary, September 13th 1787)

It would not be surprising if on a quiet summer's night in the fields inland from Brancaster (sometimes called 'Brancaster Town'), the measured step of Roman soldiers could be heard by the visitor with good hearing, and an even better imagination, for Brancaster is steeped in Roman history. The name may have derived from 'Bran' the ancient British God of the Underworld, or possibly from an old word for crow—so 'crow-fort'; to the Romans it was Branodunum. Brancaster was one of a series of 'forts of the Saxon shore', a fort and an outpost linking through Holme with Burgh Le Marsh in Lincolnshire, across The Wash. The configuration of The Wash area was probably quite different at that time and there was possibly a causeway as well as a sea ferry link.

To add to the story, there are really two Brancasters, two villages linked by a name and separated by two miles, and quite different histories. The little village of Burnham Deepdale (see p.58) was essentially a closer bed-fellow with the other Brancaster, the fishermen's village of Brancaster Staithe.

Brancaster's Roman past, as Branodunum, is reflected in its village sign, with sea horses linking the villages.

Yachts at Brancaster.

49

An atmospheric scene at Brancaster Staithe as sailors, young and old, prepare for an evening trip.

The Roman fort of Branodunum was constructed in the 4th century at Rack Hill, Brancaster, the most northerly of a line of posts as defence against the Saxons. It was for a time garrisoned by a cohort of Dalmatian cavalry under the Count of the Saxon shore. The fort was constructed as a square of about 570 feet each side with entrances at the east and west. Various Roman finds have been made including a statue of Mercury, and quantities of local oyster shells were also found here.

Before the Norman Conquest, the Lord of the Manor of Brancaster was the Abbot of Ramsay, and this continued until the Dissolution of the Monasteries. The Abbot had the right of wrecks and one Abbot even claimed a beached whale as a wreck!

The Royal West Norfolk Golf Club, a genuine 'links', was founded in 1897 and benefited from the almost-immediate royal patronage of the then Prince of Wales, later Edward VII. It must be one of the few clubs where ornithology and golf can be very much enjoyed together – and also unusual, to say the least, in that tidal flooding at times cuts off access to the clubhouse! Its Victorian clubhouse is 'a magnificent step back in time', but is situated virtually on the sea-shore.

One of England's smallest listed buildings – an old AA phone box on the main coast road.

Brancaster Staithe in earlier times was a flourishing harbour, with coal brought into the port in large barges called 'billy boys'. Local fishing from the Staithe included that for oysters in the 'oyster smacks'. They dredged for the shellfish, and put the young oysters in a 'lay' to hold them. Sole, flounder, dab, turbot and halibut, a kind of skate called 'thornback', mackerel, herring, mullet and sea trout were all caught, plus mussels and cockles. It was a busy trade, and supporting the trade, as elsewhere along this coast, would be curing houses for smoking kippers and bloaters. Flat-bottomed boats would be used for the mussels and cockles and a later addition, supported by Sheringham fishermen's expertise, was that of whelking. Smuggling was of course rife (see p.120) and Brancaster had a Coastguard Station as early as 1824. The first lifeboat, the 'Joseph and Mary', was based here in 1874. At one time, opposite the Jolly Sailors, was supposedly England's biggest malthouse.

As its name suggests this stocky turnstone finds its food by overturning stones. Several birds will often work as a team. They are surprisingly tame around humans.

THE SHIP INN

The Ship Inn, in Brancaster has a slight Nelson connection in that his old nurse, Nurse Blacket (later Mrs High), stayed here in later years with her son, the landlord of the pub. It is said that Nelson visited her there on a number of occasions. Her ghost has apparently been seen here. The fine 6 feet long ship on the outside wall is a replica of a 'ship of the line' of Nelson's time and is believed to be 100 years old. It was bought on Brentwood market and presented to the pub by a family called Cory, who had a holiday home in Brancaster.

1 The Brancaster Millennium Activity Centre, Dial House, Brancaster Staithe (01485 210719). This National Trust residential centre, is environmentally friendly (including heat-exchange from the mudflats).

2 Branodunum: the site of the Roman fort can be seen down Stockings Lane, at the extreme eastern side of the village.

3 St Mary's Brancaster is a fine church with a rare 'preacher's dial' (a very simple one-handed clock which the preacher could see and use to time his hour's sermon!). There is also a fine font cover.

4 Walks: Barrow Common is of interest. Turn right (from west) by 'The Jolly Sailors' for a road-based walk or drive. Loop back to Burnham Deepdale; Brancaster to Brancaster Staithe: down Broad Lane to finger-post on the right. Look out for mock medieval banqueting hall; Scolt Head can be seen by walking eastwards along the dunes path (approx. 1.5 miles), or the island can be visited by taking a boat trip.

5 Pubs: The Ship in Brancaster Town (01485 210333); The Jolly Sailors, 18th century (01485 210314) and The White Horse (01485 210262) are both in Brancaster Staithe.

The Dial House on Brancaster Staithe has been , amongst other things, a pub and a customs house. Today it is a National Trust activity centre.

Left: *Sea lavender carpets the salt marshes every August with a shimmering sheet of mauve.*

Right: *The model ship on the wall of the pub in Brancaster is reputed to be 100 years old.*

8 – The Burnhams

This is the happiest day of my life; what a happy day, too, for Burnham Thorpe, for it is the day of their fair.
(Horatio Nelson, on going into battle at Trafalgar, 21st October 1805)

Burnham means 'the village on a stream (burn)', the stream being the River Burn. The problem of just how many villages have the name 'Burnham' is very difficult to decide. It is largely concerned with counting parishes or settlements and at what date you make the count, as some churches no longer exist. If you ask the locals you may get several different answers. Get your map out and see how many you find! Originally the River Burn was tidal inland as far as South Creake and would have been, therefore, a more substantial waterway than it is today. It flows in a northerly direction towards the sea west of Burnham Overy Staithe. This became a busy port with ships from around the British coast and from the Low Countries calling and trading here. In addition to this, men-of-war were often to be seen in the harbour, and the port flourished until the 19th century.

Surprisingly, sea holly is a member of the carrot family.

Burnham Overy Staithe is perennially popular with sailors young and old. The young Nelson learned to sail here.

The unusual belfry of St Clement's church Burnham Overy Town.

Burnham Norton Church, in whose churchyard Captain Richard Woodget of the 'Cutty Sark' is buried, stands in an isolated position some distance from the village it serves. The original medieval village was much nearer.

From the end of the Middle Ages a change in the tide patterns and currents caused silt and debris from the Lincolnshire coast to be deposited along the north Norfolk coast forming the massive sand and shingle bank of Scolt Head across the mouth of the river Burn and this, along with the coming of the railways, caused the closure of the port. It ceased trading in the 1920s. Today it is a yachting and boating centre, with the marshes around and beyond the harbour being a haven for wildlife. In summer it is bustling with activity, and in the winter it is more peaceful with wading birds in the creeks and the call of the curlew out on the marshes. The Burnhams would have gained their wealth and prosperity from the port at the mouth of the river as it provided easy export facilities for agricultural products. Imported items such as timber and coal, needed by the local communities, were brought in through the port.

The church of St Clement at Burnham Overy Town was originally Norman and cruciform in shape having a tower at the crossing. The transepts were replaced in the 13th century by side aisles. On the wall opposite the door is an ancient wall-painting of St Christopher, the patron saint of travellers and sailors. It is fitting therefore that the graveyard should contain many graves of sailors and sea-captains.

Burnham Thorpe is a small village whose wide green is overlooked by brick and flint Georgian buildings and a 13th century church. It is the Burnham which is the furthest inland but it has a famous connection with the sea. It was in the mid 18th century that one Edmund Nelson, a Norfolk man from East Bradenham, was appointed Rector of All Saints church. Edmund had married Catherine Suckling, a great niece of Sir Robert Walpole. One of Walpole's titles was the Earl of Orford and the living at Burnham Thorpe was in the gift of the Earls of Orford. Catherine bore Edmund eleven children, and three years after Edmund's appointment, in 1758, Catherine gave birth to their sixth child, a son named Horatio (the young Nelson called himself Horace). Horatio went on to become England's most famous naval hero. After many years fighting the French navy Admiral Lord Nelson finally crushed the French fleet at the Battle of Trafalgar on 21st October 1805 but paid for his victory with his life.

Preparing for the water, at Burnham Overy Staithe.

Nelson's church at Burnham Thorpe with churchwarden and organist, Mary Heather – plus Clydo and Bonnie.

As a young boy Nelson no doubt played with boats on the River Burn and would also go to Burnham Overy Staithe to watch the ships in the harbour and hear the tall tales of seamen waiting for their next passage. Horatio was nine years old when his mother died, leaving Edmund to bring up eight surviving children, with ages ranging from 14 years old to eight months. Edmund was not a wealthy man and so needed to find positions for his older children to relieve the pressure of such a large family. When Horatio was twelve his father persuaded his wife's brother, Maurice Suckling, a sea captain, to take Horatio to sea with him. Captain Suckling regarded young Horatio as a weakling and is quoted as saying, 'What has poor Horatio done, who is so weak, that he, above all the rest, should be sent to rough it out at sea? But let him come, and the first time we go into action a cannon-ball may knock off his head and provide for him at once'. So it was, in spite of his uncle's misgivings that Horatio joined the *Raisonnable* as a midshipman, and began his colourful career in the navy.

Horatio Nelson returned, with his wife Fanny, the former Mrs Nesbitt, to live in Burnham Thorpe whilst his naval career was in the 'doldrums' from 1787 to 1793. His attachment to the village had always been strong and when in 1798 he was raised to the peerage, he took the title of Baron Nelson of the Nile and Burnham Thorpe. Again, in 1804, he wrote, 'Most probably I shall never see dear, dear Burnham again, but I have satisfaction in thinking that my bones will probably be laid with my fathers in the village that gave me birth'. However, this was not to be; he was such a popular hero that after he died at Trafalgar, he was given a state funeral and was laid to rest in St Paul's Cathedral.

The chancel arch cross made of timber from HMS Victory.

The church of All Saints was restored in the 19th century in Nelson's honour and contains much Nelson memorabilia. The cross in the chancel arch and the lectern are both made of timber from *HMS Victory*, his flagship at the Battle of Trafalgar. At the west end of the church is the crest from the World War II battleship *HMS Nelson* and her white ensigns are in the western arch of the tower. Nelson's mother and father are both buried in the chancel in front of the altar. The old font of Purbeck marble in which the infant Horatio was christened is still in use and is at the western end of the nave. The exterior east end of the church is interesting with a chequerboard design made of alternate panels of black flint and white limestone.

The largest of the Burnhams today is Burnham Market which lies about one mile to the north-west of Burnham Thorpe. It has a large green flanked by gracious 18th century houses and shops selling everything from antiques to books and shellfish to ladies' hats!

The popular, award-winning Hoste Arms is a 17th century hostelry.

Burnham Market has become a haunt for the affluent of London and the south-east and so has become known as 'Chelsea-on-Sea'. There is an up-market feel to the place but do not let that put you off paying the village a visit. A stream called the Goose Beck flows intermittently through the town centre.

Standing at the western end of the green is the Hoste Arms Hotel. Originally called the Pitt Arms it was built around 1640 but changed its name in 1811 after Sir William Hoste, one of Nelson's protégés, won a victory at Lissa when he flew the signal, 'Remember Nelson!'.

Less than a mile north-west of Burnham Market is the small settlement of Burnham Norton. From the high point, near the church, are wonderful views over the Burnham marshes towards Scolt Head Island to the north. The church of St Margaret has one of the most complete round towers in Norfolk built between 1000 and 1066. In 1241 a Carmelite Friary was built nearby and around this time the church was enlarged in the early English style. The Norman font is low and has an unusual trellis design on the side panels. The painted screen dates from 1458. It also has a very fine hexagonal pulpit. In the churchyard is the grave of master-mariner Captain Woodget who was master of the famous tea-clipper the *Cutty Sark*. The *Cutty Sark* can be seen at Greenwich in London.

This Burnham Market fish shop is one of the many in North Norfolk selling local sea-food.

A unique Norman calendar font depicting the labours throughout the year. May's banner and branches represent rogation-tide: June shows weeding: July is mowing (or hoeing): August shows binding a corn sheaf.

The most westerly of the Burnhams is Burnham Deepdale. This little village lies between the sea and the marshes to the north and farmland to the south. Again the church offers much of interest. It is dedicated to St Mary and it has a round tower which predates the Norman Conquest. Inside is a square Norman font of Barnack stone and its faces depict the year from a farming man's point of view. For example, September, threshing and December, feasting. The church also has a collection of medieval stained glass.

Burnham Westgate and Burnham Ulph cum Sutton are really parts of Burnham Market. Westgate is at the western entrance to the village and Ulph at the east. Sutton, meaning South Town was absorbed into the parish of Ulph.

The Burnhams provide much for the visitor to see and there are good walks in the surrounding countryside and on the marshes. Indeed it makes a pleasant walk to park the car at one of the Burnhams and visit some or all of the others on foot.

This fine, tower mill situated by the coast road a little out of the village of Burnham Overy Staithe is now under the control of the National Trust.

THINGS TO DO

❶ **Burnham Market:** old Georgian town with many fine buildings and interesting shops.

❷ **Burnham Norton Church:** unusual font, painted screen and grave of the master of the Cutty Sark.

❸ **Burnham Thorpe Church:** plenty of Nelson memorabilia. Interesting chequerboard design on the outside of the east end.

❹ **Walks:** a circular walk south from Burnham Thorpe using the lanes: start from the church; a walk from Burnham Market visiting Burnham Overy Town and Burnham Norton, about 4.5 miles: start from the green; the Norfolk Coast Path from Burnham Deepdale to Burnham Overy Staithe.

❺ **TIC:** at Deepdale Farm, Burnham Deepdale (01485 210256).

❻ **Pubs and eating places:** Burnham Market, Hoste Arms (01328 738 777) coaching inn dating from 1550, with Nelson connections, The Lord Nelson (01328 738321), Fishe's Restaurant for seafood (01328 738588) all in Burnham Market. The Lord Nelson, (01328 738241) Burnham Thorpe; The Hero, (01328 738334), Burnham Overy Staithe.

9 – Scolt Head and Holkham

I had rather remain the first of the ducks than the last of the geese.
(Thomas Coke when asked if he would like a peerage)

The Norfolk coast is ever changing, not just in its moods as the seasons and the weather change but in its very structure. Material has been transported down the Lincolnshire coast and sediment has built up against the North Norfolk coast. Scolt Head Island is a product of this. It is steadily growing in a westward direction and is a prime example of an offshore barrier island. It is part of the North Norfolk Coast SSSI. It is a National Nature Reserve owned jointly by the National Trust and the Norfolk Wildlife Trust and managed, under lease, by English Nature. Scolt Head is a non-intervention reserve where the natural coastal processes are allowed to occur.

The pink-footed goose (above) *is a winter visitor to this area. The ringed plover* (below) *is a resident bird, plentiful in numbers round this coast. They feed on small insects, molluscs and worms.*

The habitats are dunes, tidal sand, mudflats, shingle and saltmarsh. The reserve is largely undisturbed because of the problems of access. Ferries operate from Brancaster Staithe and Burnham Overy Staithe from April to September. It is internationally important, with large numbers of breeding terns, mainly sandwich terns, and wintering wildfowl and waders.

The vegetation, which can similarly be found further along the coast at Blakeney Point, is made up of plants such as sea campion, bird's-foot trefoil, sea bindweed, sea holly and shrubby seablite.

Dogs are not allowed from mid-April to mid-August and at other times only on leads. Due to the sensitivity of the island, access is only permitted to specified areas, which vary during the season. There are no facilities on the island, no disabled access to it, and it can only be reached from the places mentioned above. On no account should visitors attempt to cross the mud-flats to reach the island.

Holkham also has a National Nature Reserve which stretches from Burnham Norton to Blakeney and covers about 4,000 hectares. Access is by footpath from the main

Scolt Head Island is largely owned by the National Trust.

A feature of Holkham Bay is the ring of Corsican pine, planted by the Coke family. There are smaller numbers of three other species.

settlements along this route or from the three car parks which are at Burnham Overy Staithe (free), at Lady Ann's Drive, Holkham (pay) and Wells Beach Road (pay). See Tourist Information for details. Holkham Bay is a fine, sandy beach surrounded by dunes and pine woods. It is at the end of Lady Ann's Drive.

The Coke family have lived on the Holkham Estate since Elizabethan times when Sir Edward Coke was Attorney General to Elizabeth I and Chief Justice to James I. The present Palladian style hall was built by Thomas Coke , 1st Earl of Leicester, between 1734 and 1764. The house, set in 3,000 acres of parkland, is constructed in local yellow brick and has a magnificent entrance hall of English alabaster.

The house is open to the public and the site also contains a Bygones Museum, a Pottery and a Garden Centre. There are many walks to be taken in the park and large numbers of wildfowl can be seen on the mile-long lake. Around the estate you will also see some of the 600 fallow deer. The much-restored 13th century church of St Withburga can be seen, about one mile west from the house. It stands on what was the site of the medieval village of Holkham. The original port with its staithe was close to the present Victoria Hotel.

THOMAS COKE , 1ST EARL OF LEICESTER 1752-1842
'COKE OF NORFOLK'

After his 'Grand Tour', the building of the present Hall, and a career in Parliament, the 1st Earl of Leicester retired to the life of a country squire and decided to farm his own land. He followed 'Turnip' Townshend's crop rotation methods but he is best remembered for the introduction of Southdown sheep to the county, finally having a flock of 2500 on the estate. He set up the Holkham 'Sheep Shearing', a great agricultural event that was held regularly for the next 43 years and attracted people from all over the world. The park bustled with farmers who went on farm walks, observed the sheep shearing and inspected prize beasts and new implements. It was the forerunner of the modern Agricultural Show. When Thomas Coke died, a large monument to him was erected at the north end of the lake.

Holkham Hall, seat of the Earls of Leicester, is a fine Palladian mansion, gracing the north Norfolk coast.

A herd of fallow deer resting in the afternoon sun in Holkham Park.

The wide open vista of Holkham Bay, chosen for the final sequence of the film 'Shakespeare in Love'.

Cord-grass is a vigorous natural hybrid which binds the mud and begins saltmarsh formation.

THINGS TO DO

❶ Bygones Museum: old agricultural implements and much more. Free 'History of Farming' exhibition. (01328 710227).

❷ Holkham Art, Crafts & Fine Food Centre (01328 710227).

❸ Holkham Hall: 18th century Palladian Mansion; boat trips on the lake (01328 710227).

❹ Holkham Pottery: (01328 710227).

❺ St Withburga's Church Holkham Park.

❻ Scolt Head Island: for a visit contact English Nature (01603 598400). Car parking at Burnham Overy Staithe.

❼ Walks: Scolt Head Island (see above); Holkham Park: 'The Lake Walk' from the car park at the North Gate; 'The Farm Walk' from the car park at the South Gate; 'The Park Walk' from the almshouses by the North Gate (01328 710227).

❽ Pubs and eating places: The Victoria Hotel adjacent to the North Gate (01328 711008); The Stables Café Holkham Hall (01328 710227).

Wells-next-the-Sea to Weybourne

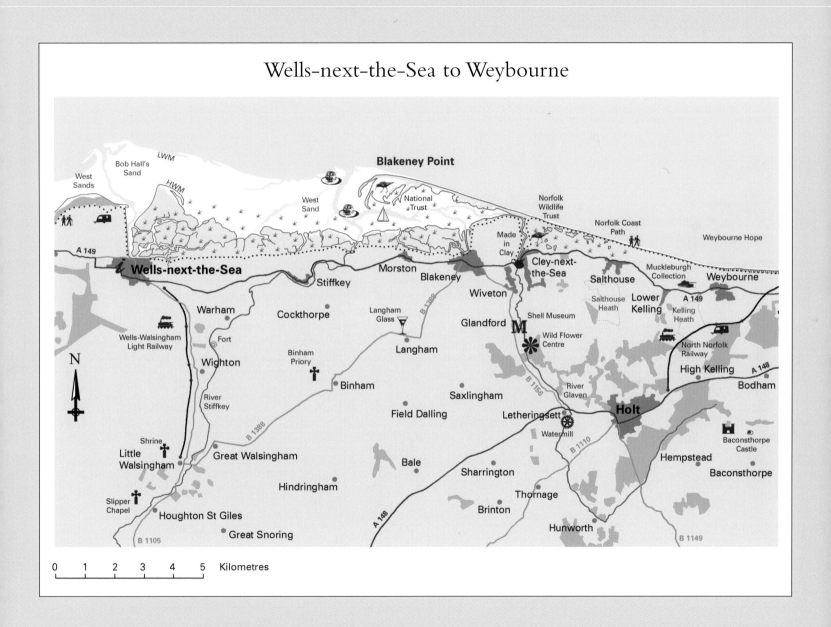

Blakeney Point

LWM

West Sands

Bob Hall's Sand

HWM

West Sand

National Trust

Norfolk Wildlife Trust

Norfolk Coast Path

Weybourne Hope

A 149

Made in Clay

Wells-next-the-Sea

Morston

Stiffkey

Blakeney

Cley-next-the-Sea

Salthouse

Muckleburgh Collection

Weybourne

Wiveton

Warham

Cockthorpe

Langham Glass

Glandford

M

Shell Museum

Salthouse Heath

Lower Kelling

Kelling Heath

A 149

Wells-Walsingham Light Railway

Fort

Wild Flower Centre

North Norfolk Railway

High Kelling

A 148

Binham Priory

Langham

Wighton

Binham

Saxlingham

River Glaven

Bodham

River Stiffkey

B 1388

Field Dalling

B 1156

Letheringsett

Holt

Shrine

Little Walsingham

Great Walsingham

Bale

Watermill

B 1110

Hempstead

Baconsthorpe Castle

Hindringham

Sharrington

Thornage

Baconsthorpe

Slipper Chapel

Houghton St Giles

Great Snoring

A 148

Brinton

Hunworth

B 1149

B 1105

N

0 1 2 3 4 5   Kilometres

Wells is a busy and popular harbour

10 – Wells-next-the-Sea

When I came on deck, Mr Bligh was standing afore the mizzen mast with his hands tied behind –
and Christian hold of him by the cord with one hand and a bayonet in the other hand.
(John Fryer's Journal)

Wells-next-the-Sea has been a port of no mean calibre for centuries and a town where tourism and commerce have gone hand in hand. As well as the necessary tourist gift shops, ice-cream parlours and cafes that overlook the water, there are also elegant Georgian shop fronts in Staithe Street and High Street for example, and a delightful area called The Buttland, up the hill from the harbour, more reminiscent of a cathedral close. The name 'Buttland' (earlier 'Butland') refers to waste ground, and in this case there is no evidence of an archery connection, as is so often the case.

The town was originally called Guella and the Anglo-Saxons called it Wylla; by the 14th century it had become Welles, derived, as the name suggests, from the many clear springs locally. The history of Wells over the centuries is inextricably bound with the sea, and this stretches back to at least the 13th century. Later, in the 16th and 17th centuries local fishermen took part in the distant Iceland trade, and suffered at the hands of the Hanseatic pirates; the latter in one incident were reported as capturing several boats out of Wells. An interesting entry in Wells' burial records from the Tudor period blamed 'an execrable witch of King's Lynn', one Mother Gabley, for the deaths of a number of seamen. In the 17th century concerns were expressed that 'the quay or landing place of the port is at this present become very ruinous'. A levy of 6d on a ton of goods was made for 'the better preserving of the quay, creeks, channel and landing place of Wells'. A 'Haven Man' was also appointed at this time.

Some of the gracious period houses which surround the central, grassy area of The Buttland.

This memorial commemorates the tragic loss of 11 crewmen from the 'Eliza Adams' lifeboat, in 1880.

Locally, Wells has always been associated with whelk fishing in the open-decked clinker-built whelkers, fishing the whelk beds with round black-roped whelk pots; the metal bases were constructed by the local blacksmiths. Whelks have provided Wells with a staple fishing diet over the years, together with sprat, herring and winkles. The whelks were cooked in whelk coppers, then put into hessian sacks; at the heyday of the industry a special rail loop was created by the LNER to serve the town. The growth of the railways adversely affected the shipping trade but brought the tourists as compensation for some people. The loss of shipbuilding, the movement away from the land and emigrate all affected Wells' population in the nineteenth century.

Wells' quay was originally lined with granaries, with their unloading hoists, and the evidence is still there to see. Cargoes of corn and sugar-beet left from here, and coal might be unloaded; large 200 ton ships would have been seen. In the mid 19th century there

Yachts at rest against a stormy sky.

66

THE MUTINY ON THE BOUNTY

Wells has a direct link with the Mutiny on the *Bounty*, being the birthplace of John Fryer, master of the Bounty. Fryer remained loyal to Captain Bligh and apparently (in Fryer's account) tried to stop the 1789 mutiny when Fletcher Christian took over from its captain William Bligh. Fryer's young brother-in-law Richard Tinkler was also on that voyage, and both of them were included in the group of sailors that was set adrift in a 23 foot ship's boat. They were at sea for 36 days and covered almost 4000 miles. Partly thanks to Captain Bligh's navigational skills both Fryer and Tinkler lived to tell the tale in their home town of Wells. Bligh suffered three mutinies and his account of this one was quite different from Fryer's.

A plaque commemorating Wells' link with the mutiny on the Bounty.

were as many as 12 harbour pilots. The original harbour was nearer the sea, but the coastline has changed over the centuries. Today the lifeboat house is found a mile from the town. The lifeboat tradition has always been a strong one at Wells, and particularly so because of a terrible disaster in 1880 that united the town in grief. The first lifeboat, the *Eliza Adams*, capsized and 11 of the 13 crew were lost. A memorial commemorates the event. During the last war, Wells lifeboatmen were so often needed, they slept in their boathouse on a rota basis, and were ready to support returning aircraft in difficulties.

The present church of St Nicholas (patron saint of children and fishermen) is a re-building of the original church of 1460. In 1879, during a terrible storm the church was struck by lightning and almost completely destroyed. The rebuilding was completed in 1883.

In former times, when fairs were more exuberant perhaps, barrels of burning tar were rolled down Staithe Street into the water, and of course the traditional regattas might last for days and include the famous 'greasy-pole' challenge, the aim being to walk the treacherous pole without falling into the water.

A bed of wild flowers along the bank to the lifeboat house, containing wild carrot, black horehound, mallow and viper's bugloss.

Holiday purchases on the harbour front.

A timeless study of water and boats.

The present tidal estuary is surrounded by salt marshes that are often covered at high tide. The Wells' marshes are important for bird life and also the three-mile stretch of pines to the west of the sea wall (completed in 1859) has become a mecca for bird-watchers. Since the early 1970s an impressive list of rare migrants has been credited to these woods in the winter months. Wells is associated with brent and pink-footed geese, the latter in numbers at times exceeding 100,000. They can often be observed from the quay. As with most of the coast, but especially in the area towards Holkham, local knowledge must be sought before venturing from marked paths onto tidal sands. 'Abraham's Bosom' slightly west of the town, is a popular area for visitors and locals, and provides a boating area.

The brent goose is the smallest of the European geese. The darker bellied variety flies to southern British estuaries in close-packed flocks.

Colourful beach-huts provide an enjoyable base for exploring Wells' open sands.

❶ **TIC**, Staithe Street (01328 710885) .

❷ **Walks:** along the bank to the lifeboat shed, about a mile, and beyond this past the beach huts; to Abraham's Bosom, an earlier harbour that is now a secluded boating place. From here you may continue through the pines to Holkham Gap. Check on tides for these walks.

❸ **Wells' Harbour Railway** can be used for the outward or return journey to Abraham's Bosom or Wells' beach.

❹ **Pubs** worth a visit are the 'Bowling Green' (01328 710100), opposite the church, or 'The Crown', accommodation (01328 710209) on the Buttlands. In the mid-nineteenth century there were 32 pubs! There are plenty of good alternatives to these in the town, or good tea shops such as Nelson's in Staithe Street.

❺ **'Worth a Detour':** The Wells and Walsingham Light Railway opened in 1982. Its four miles make it the longest 10.25 inch narrow-gauge railway (01328 711630) in the world. Walsingham was England's premier shrine during the Middle Ages, and is certainly worth a rail or car excursion for a few hours. It is a most unusual village, steeped in history, but with several good pubs and tea shops to sustain you. It even has a tiny Russian Orthodox Church in a converted railway station, two current shrines, and the remains of an enormous priory and a smaller friary.

A tranquil combination of pastel colours in the High Street. This street of delightful period houses is a 'must' for a walking tour of Wells.

A little loving attention to the narrow gauge loco on the Wells to Walsingham light railway.

11 – Stiffkey and Morston

*The sea was half a mile from the village, and the field ended in a plantation of land – a fringe of
stunted trees, and then steeply down to a pebbly shore and a creek where a fisherman's boat was moored.
We sat down on the grass, gazing out over the marshes, one vast gut-channeled prairie of pale blue sea-lavender.*
(Henry Williamson, *The Story of a Norfolk Farm.*)

The West Country writer Henry Williamson settled in the pretty village of Stiffkey for a few years in 1937, in various cottages then at Old Hall Farm, becoming a farmer. He recounts his experiences in the above book. Stiffkey is an ancient village with a former estuary that until the 17th century at least, was tidal up to Warham. Romano-British pottery finds have occurred between Stiffkey and Morston, and the former is mentioned in Domesday, under the name Stivecai.

A glimpse of one of the ancient towers of Stiffkey Old Hall set close to the church of St John.

Although not open to the public, but just visible from the road and churchyard, is the fine building of Stiffkey Old Hall, planned and partially built (on much earlier foundations) by Sir Nicholas Bacon, Keeper of the Great Seal to Queen Elizabeth I. He left detailed instructions to his son Nathaniel as to how he wished the building of the hall to proceed, but very little cash to back up the grand plans. £200 even at that time was a relatively modest amount for a grand building. Sir Nicholas wanted a four-sided house built around a courtyard with four towers at the external corners and four more at the internal corners. It was to have a series of gardens mathematically planned in relation to the shape of the house. Building began in 1576, but when Sir Nicholas died the plans were modified and the house was completed in 1604. Certain demolition was undertaken in the late 17th century to reduce the upkeep and certain refitting work in the following century; it remains a fascinating piece of architecture. The hall was let for three years to Richard Hughes, author of 'A High Wind in Jamaica'.

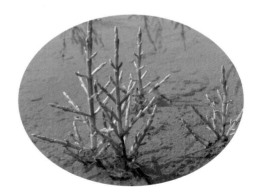

Samphire can be gathered from the bare mud and either eaten raw or cooked as the 'poor man's asparagus'.

There were two separate manors in Stiffkey from the Norman Conquest (William the Conqueror was lord of the manor for a time) until Sir Nicholas united them in 1573. There were also two churches in the same churchyard, St John's and St Mary's. A mound is all that remains of the latter. In the 17th century Stiffkey was the centre locally for growing saffron, a valuable crop to harvest. Kilns for drying the saffron would have been present in the village.

The writer Henry Williamson lived for a time in this cottage in Stiffkey.

Stiffkey was also the home of Revd. Harold Davidson, whose story back in the 1930s made the national newspapers. It is a bizarre and somewhat sad tale. Like an earlier and eminent predecessor, William Gladstone, Revd. Davidson had a mission to save girls from prostitution. Like Gladstone his motives were misunderstood, some would say deliberately. Innocent and naïve he may have been, but the newspapers hounded him and in its wisdom the Church of England defrocked him. He and his wife and five children left his beloved Stiffkey. In a desire to raise money to clear his name, Harold Davidson entered the fairground circuit at Blackpool, preaching his sermons to large, often jeering, crowds. At Skegness he chose to speak from a lion's cage. He was badly mauled and died shortly afterwards. He had always hoped to return to his village totally exonerated. It has to be said that parishioners of that generation in the village will hear nothing against him. To them he was always 'Little Jimmy' and to the newspapers 'the prostitutes' padre'. It was estimated that 3,000 mourners followed his coffin.

Stiffkey's lamp shop is an Aladdin's cave for browsers. It has been in business for almost 30 years.

Hundreds of visitors each year take one of the seal boats and head for Blakeney Point.

Another claim to fame is a particular shellfish, a cockle called a 'Stewkey Blue' (Stewkey being the local variant of Stiffkey). The sad background to their collection was the permanently bent backs of the cockle girls who gave their health to the collection of these shellfish. The village sign shows cockle gatherers within the circular frame of a cockle shell with the old name 'Stewkey'.

Morston is one of the starting points for boat trips to Blakeney Point to get a close view of the seal population. These must surely be some of the most photographed and feted seals in the country with a regular fleet of boats from Morston and Blakeney passing by for most of the year.

The pretty village of Morston, looking towards the Manor House.

The Church of All Saints today has a somewhat patchwork look. After being struck by lightning in 1743 a major rebuilding of a section of its stone tower was carried out in red brick, in the days before people were sensitive to the guidelines of restoration work. Inside, the small church is a delight, with its hanging chandeliers, and the magnificent 15th century painted screen. The building dates from the 12th to the 15th centuries. The creeks and muddy pathways of Morston with rickety bridges and staithes are worth exploring at any time of the year, and there is an abundance of bird and plant life present. Even the simplest natural features such as the 'crazy paving' effects of the mud as it dries out, or the flotsam and jetsam of old pots and nets are a constant source of interest. The National Trust administers the area, providing the facility of an observation tower for keen ornithologists, and refreshments to sustain the weary! Sails are always present somewhere on the horizon and there is no better spot to encounter Norfolk's wide open skies. The view towards Blakeney from Morston is much painted and photographed.

THINGS TO DO

❶ Explore the muddy creeks and pathways of Morston marshes, (NT car-park, observation tower and refreshments) with its richness of bird and plant life.

❷ Henry Williamson's former cottage in Stiffkey has been identified with a plaque by the 'Henry Williamson Society'. Approaching the village from the west it is immediately beyond the lamp shop and antique centre, on the same side.

❸ Seal trips to Blakeney Point can be booked in Morston (or Blakeney): Temple's Bean's and Bishop's are three firms running them.

❹ Walks: Norfolk Coastal Path is easily accessible at Stiffkey. As you approach the village from the west, take the left-hand turn named 'Greenway', shortly after the village sign. There is a NT car park at the end of this lane. From here the walk to Morston along the edge of the marshes is 2.75 miles and to Wells is 3.25 miles (car shuttle or return); over the bridge in the village centre, heading inland from the coast road is the start of a marked country walk of just over a mile; from the National Trust Centre head right along the National Rivers Authority sea wall towards Blakeney (1.25 miles).

❺ Pubs and eating places: Stiffkey has the 16th century 'Red Lion' (01328 830552) and Morston has 'Morston Hall' (Jacobean times) (01263 741041), or 'The Anchor' (01263 741392). The latter has been in the Temple family for over a century.

Hundreds of visitors each year take one of the seal boats and head for Blakeney Point.

Temple's and Bean's seal boat trips can be booked in the village of Morston.

❻ 'Worth a detour' is the village of Cockthorpe, the home of Admiral Sir Cloudesley Shovel (c1650-1707). He came from a poor background and was apprenticed to a shoemaker. He ran away to sea as cabin boy to Sir John Narbrough (1640-1688) who like Sir Cloudesley, was also christened in Cockthorpe Church. Sir Cloudsley rose rapidly in the navy but sadly perished when his ship foundered with all hands, off the Scilly Isles. He is buried in Westminster Abbey. Also in Cockthorpe Church (key opposite) is a monument to Sir James Calthorpe and his wife Barbara. It is recorded that the latter, aged 86 years 'was much comforted by the sight of 193 of her children and their offspring'.

❼ 'Worth a detour' for historians is Warham Camp, just inland from Stiffkey. It is an Iron Age camp associated with the Iceni tribe and is a double-banked earthwork. The western end, containing the original entrance, was destroyed when the River Stiffkey's course was rerouted. It is not easy to find. The road south out of Warham goes over a bridge. A few hundred yards after this take a right hand gate and the track leads to the camp. While near Warham, why not give the Thee Horseshoes a try.

12 – Blakeney and Cley-next-the-Sea

'I'm doing a series of articles for an American magazine,' I said. 'Historical stuff. I was over at St Margaret's at Cley yesterday.'
'A beautiful church.' He sat down in the nearest pew. 'Forgive me, I tire rather easily these days.'
'There's a table tomb in the churchyard there,' I went on. 'Perhaps you know it? "To James Greeve"'.

Jack Higgins, *The Eagle has Landed.*

Blakeney was a port from the Middle Ages until the last century. Today it is one of the most popular villages along the Norfolk coast. The village is recorded in the Domesday Book as Esnuterle which later became corrupted to Snitterley. Later the haven and village, in the lee of a shingle bank known as 'Blakeney', took this name.

Near this point on the coast the River Glaven enters the sea and Blakeney stands on one of the interconnecting channels which cut through the marshes. The port exported cereals and malt and imported coal, timber and iron. In the 13th century it ranked fourth in the top ten ports in the country and at that time was used by royalty when visiting the Low Countries, it being a fairly short crossing to that part of the continent.

Blakeney harbour, always a popular place to visit.

One of the larger boats seen at Blakeney, the good ship Juno.

Cley mill in its various moods.

By the 19th century the problem of silting, which affected the whole of the north Norfolk coast, was acute at the mouth of the Glaven. In 1817 the Blakeney Harbour Company was set up to regulate trade and improve the harbour. An Act of Parliament, was passed which allowed the Board to cut new channels and nearly £2,000 was spent on this work. The eminent engineer, Thomas Telford, submitted a scheme but it was not taken up. Four years later an Enclosure Act was passed and banks and sluices were placed in such a way to give Blakeney a new lease of life but at the expense of Cley which went into decline, just as Wiveton had done 200 years earlier. All this came too late; with the coming of the railways to the nearby town of Holt and the continuous problem of silting, the port was doomed.

Today Blakeney is reliant upon the tourist trade. Its bustling quay is bordered by picturesque flint cottages. In the narrow streets they huddle against the north-east winds. Leave the car at the quay and explore the village on foot.

On the high ground at the landward side of the village stands the beautiful church of St Nicholas. The chancel is older than the rest of the church. The former dates from the 13th century, having been built by the Carmelite Friars and is a fine example of Early English architecture. A hundred or so years later the town had become prosperous enough to build the present nave and tower. The church is unique in having a small additional tower at the eastern end of the church. It once served as a lighthouse to guide the ships into the harbour but it is thought to have originally been a stair turret to gain access to a room over the chancel.

The distinctive 'booming' of the bittern can be heard in Norfolk's reed beds, such as at Cley

NORFOLK NATURALISTS TRUST

In 1926 a group of forward thinking naturalists formed the Norfolk Naturalists Trust, (subsequently renamed the Norfolk Wildlife Trust) to ensure that the Cley marshes would be managed correctly in perpetuity. Thus the Cley Reserve is the oldest county nature reserve in Britain. Today the trust is still strong and cares for more than 50 sites of special interest in Norfolk. The idea spread and there is now a nationwide network of trusts catering and caring for the wildlife that inhabits our islands. The country now has some 47 local Wildlife Trusts caring for over 2,560 nature reserves and with a membership of 413,000.

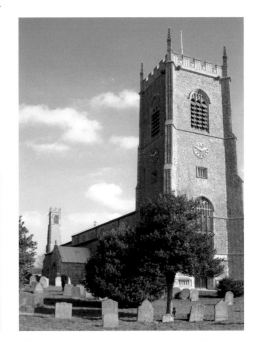

The church of St Nicholas in Blakeney with its unusual lantern tower.

A popular stop for fresh fish.

Whalebone House is very unusual for its decorative front combining flints with bones (sheep not whales!).

Tourists come here to visit Blakeney Point, a spit of sand and shingle which can be traced eastwards as far as Weybourne cliffs. The Cley Reserve is the oldest county nature reserve in Britain (see information box). This part of the coast has been designated an Area of Outstanding Natural Beauty and the marshes and wide open spaces around the Point make it a haven for birds and wildlife. The area is owned and managed by the National Trust. Access is by foot from Cley (a round trip of seven miles or so) or by ferry from Blakeney or Morston according to the tides. Besides the many birds, which can be seen, including terns, there are also colonies of common and grey seals. There is of course restricted access during the main bird breeding season.

Continue east along the A149 and you will come to Cley-next-the-sea (Cley rhymes with 'eye'). Cley today is a quiet photogenic Norfolk village with rugged flint houses, narrow alleys and a rather larger church than one would expect, that is until you unpeel the layers of history and reveal Cley's important past.

Cley along with Wiveton and Blakeney made up the three Glaven ports which were important during the Middle Ages. You can only really visit Cley on foot. Cars can be left at the Village Hall car park. The church, which stands at the opposite end of the village to the windmill, is dedicated to St Margaret of Antioch. It stands on the site of an earlier church and was planned on a grand scale. Cley and its landowners were extremely rich in the 14th century. Unfortunately the Black Death reached the area and killed off the majority of the population as well as the master masons working on the church. The east end was not built with the same opulence as the main body of the church.

If you stand outside the present church and look across the green towards Wiveton church then the area in front of you is where the original busy and bustling ports of Cley and Wiveton were. Cley's early days were not always peaceful. In 1317 it was reported that the harbour was 'in the grip of pirates 'and in 1405 one of Cley's seamen captured the young Prince James of Scotland and passed him over to Henry IV who kept him hostage for the next 17 years! Two hundred years later the local landowner, Sir Henry Calthorpe, without any consultation, began a reclamation scheme which entailed putting a dam across the river. Although this was demolished after petitions to the king, the damage had been done and the river silted up. Cley moved its harbour to the area around the windmill and Wiveton ceased to be a port. Cley continued to flourish until the 19th century but Blakeney's 'improvements', the silting-up along the coast and the coming of the railway to Holt, finished its trade.

Today, Cley is eminently suited to those seeking a more quiet and peaceful holiday. Walk round the village with its unchanged buildings and narrow lanes. Look out for Whalebone House, now a restaurant, whose walls have panels of flint and bone. These are not whale bones but rather sheep bones plus horses' teeth! There is also the popular Smokehouse which still cures and smokes fish in the traditional way. The old Customs House and Cley Hall are just two more examples of fascinating buildings.

The mill was built in the 18th century and ground corn until 1919. It was later converted into visitor accommodation. Regular tours are available for non-residents.

Fox hunting is not banned! On a roof boss in the church porch at Cley, an old lady is chasing a fox attacking her chickens, and throwing her distaff at it.

The 14th century church of St Margaret of Antioch.

The yellow-horned poppy is one of the few plants that grows well on shingle.

The sandwich tern (above) *is the largest of the terns visiting Britain, nesting on shingle beaches and dunes. The common tern* (below) *is a graceful bird, sometimes called the 'sea swallow'. All the birds in a colony will often take off together.*

THINGS TO DO

① **Blakeney Point:** this Nature Reserve can be reached by boat from Morston or Blakeney (see previous chapter) or by walking from Cley along the bank.

② **Blakeney Church** with its unusual twin towers, has a hammer-beam roof. Sir Henry Birkin, 1920s Bentley racing driver, is buried in the churchyard.

③ **Cley Church** has fine architectural features; pews have 'poppy head' ends and carvings of various animals and figures on the arm rests. There is also a fine Jacobean pulpit. Can you spot the 'pipe and tabor' player in the rear nave?

④ **Cley Mill** (01263 740209): 18th century mill now used for B&B and self catering accommodation. Take the opportunity if a tour is available, as Cley Mill is one of Norfolk's most popular mills.

⑤ **Walks:** follow the Norfolk Coast Path to Salthouse for exploration of the marshes with their flora and fauna, and also the fine views. Cley Village Trail: tour of the village exploring its many interesting alley ways and houses (details on the internet).

⑥ **Pubs and eating places:** The White Horse (01263 740574), The Blakeney Hotel, (01263 740797) a harbour front hotel with stunning views; The King's Arms Hotel, (01263 740341): look out for the date in the tiles on the roof, all in Blakeney; The George, (01263 740652) a fine old Terroir Restaurant, Whalebone House, (01263 740336); The Three Swallows, (01263 740526), in Cley; The Bell (01263 740101) in Wiveton is worth trying.

⑦ **'Worth a detour':** Glandford Shell Museum (01263 740081).

The reed-fringed River Glaven looking towards Wiveton church.

13 – Salthouse, Kelling and Weybourne

If you would old England win, first at Weybourne Hope begin.
(old saying).

The small village of Salthouse nestles around the church of St Nicholas at the edge of the saltmarsh. Here there would have been salt-pans and warehouses in which to store the large piles of salt crystals and the bags ready for transport. Indeed, this is the derivation of the village's name. Today the village is famed for its wide open spaces and its wildlife. Birdwatchers come from all over the country to observe both common and rare species. To the north, between the marsh and the sea, is a vast shingle bank, the only defence from high tides and severe weather. Here you get what the locals call a 'lazy wind'; it doesn't go round you but rather straight through you! In 1953 the sea breached the bank and much damage was done to the marshes and the village. At the back of the village, to the south, the land rises quite steeply and on top of the ridge

Sea campion is a mat-forming perennial found on shingle and cliffs.

This shingle bank is the only barrier protecting the marshes from the sea.

Salthouse church and marsh from the heath.

Rosebay willow herb and ragwort growing near Salthouse.

is Salthouse Heath. This is an ancient site and the area contains Bronze Age barrows; those with a keen eye will be able to find worked flint. The heath is under management to return the site to true heathland after the invasion of trees.

Salthouse's fine church stands between the village and the common, high enough on the slope to avoid any flood-water. The nave and chancel, together with the aisles, were re-built in the 15th century at a time of great prosperity. The church contains a fine font with cuddly lions at the base and a screen which has been removed to the rear of the building.

To the east is the attractive village of Kelling which has been spared much modern development but the only building of any antiquity is Beck House which dates from the 17th century. Kelling in the past had a reputation for smuggling and there is a record of a skirmish in 1833 between the excisemen and smugglers on the beach which was known as Kelling Hard. Two smugglers were injured and the excisemen captured about 1500 kg of tobacco and 500 gallons of brandy. It seems most of the village was involved, including the parson!

If you look for the church in the village you won't find it as it is up towards the Heath. The church is dedicated to St Mary the Virgin and at one time the village centred around it. It contains a rare Easter Sepulchre. Most of these were destroyed in the 16th or 17th centuries. The Sepulchre would originally have been heavily painted. On Maundy Thursday the priest would place the consecrated elements of communion in the Sepulchre and there they would remain until Easter Day when they would be removed with great ceremony, and used.

Salthouse church from the reed beds.

On the higher ground above the village is Kelling Heath, extending over 250 acres, one of the coast's 'areas of outstanding natural beauty'. It has a network of paths, including a nature trail (squirrel markers), and it is easily accessible. The North Norfolk Railway crosses the heath and there is a 'halt' where the train can be caught.

Weybourne, pronounced 'Webbon' locally, nestles in a hollow below Kelling Heath and on the top of the cliffs. The name is derived from an old English word meaning 'felon's stream'. The ruins of an Augustinian priory stand in the grounds of the 15th century church. The North Norfolk Railway station is about half a mile out of the village. This has been greatly used by TV and film companies as a 'period' location. At the eastern end of the village stands a former mill now part of a privately-owned dwelling.

The road from Kelling Heath gives this panoramic view over Weybourne.

The black-headed gull in winter plumage (left) and summer plumage (right). It is one of the commonest British resident gulls. As well as feeding inland, often following a plough, it chooses low shores, harbours and estuaries.

The brilliant yellow of oilseed rape flowers acts as colourful background to the houses of Kelling village.

At Weybourne the 'cliff section' of the Norfolk coast begins and extends eastwards to Happisburgh. These western cliffs are especially important geologically.

Down at the beach the sea-bed shelves dramatically away to deep water, known as 'Weybourne Hope'. The deep water close-in has always presented a fear of invasion, sending shivers down the spines of the locals. These fears were probably not helped by the saying: 'if you would old England win, first at Weybourne Hope begin'. The Armada, the Dutch, Napoleon Bonaparte and finally Hitler were all expected along this stretch of coast. To counter this eventuality, there has been a military camp here since Armada times. During the Second World War it was a major 'ack-ack' camp and today this houses the Muckleburgh Collection, a working military museum.

THINGS TO DO

❶ Muckleburgh Collection (01263 588210) Norfolk's largest military collection; regular demonstrations.

❷ The Poppy Line 01263 820800) is a preserved steam railway with workshops at Weybourne station. Access is at Weybourne and Kelling. Heath Halt, as well as from Sheringham on Holt.

❸ St Nicholas' Church, Salthouse: fine painted screen and scratched drawings of ships on the back of the choir stalls.

❹ Walks: on the marshes and along the shingle banks between all three villages; many walks and trails on Salthouse and Kelling Heaths, with spectacular views to the seashore, and rich natural history.

❺ Pubs and eating places: Dun Cow (01263 740467) Salthouse: open fires, exposed beams and flint walls; Cookies Crab Shop (01263 740352) tiny but very popular eating place; Ship Inn (01263 721) and Maltings Hotel (01263 588731), Weybourne: latter is a 16th century flint building; The Pheasant, (01263 588382) and The Reading Room Tea Rooms, (01263 588227), Kelling.

A Churchill tank greets visitors to the Muckleburgh Collection in Weybourne.

Sheringham to Bacton

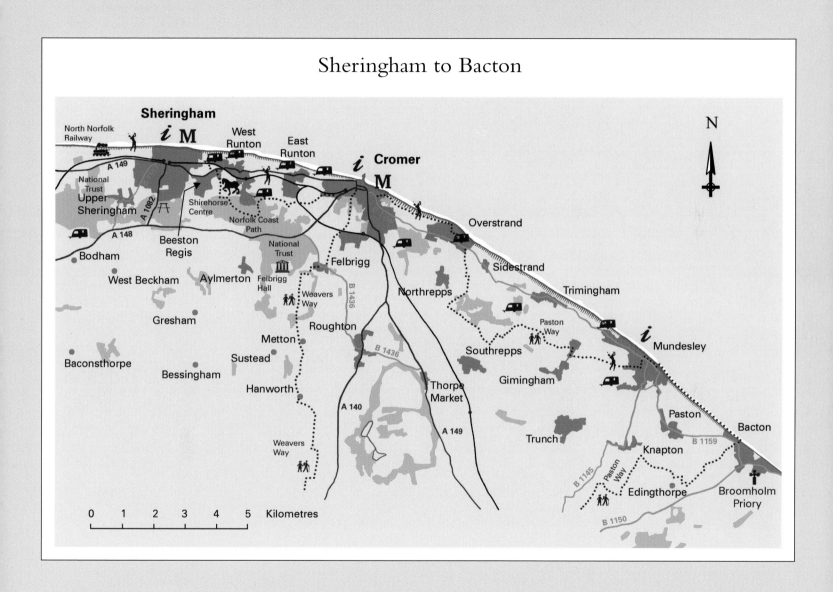

Clouds of steam fill the air on the 'Poppy Line' as the engine 'Green Arrow' passes Sheringham Golf Course en route to Weybourne.

14 – Sheringham and Beeston Regis

Our town joins upon the main sea, and we are afraid every night the enemy should come ashore and fire our town when we be in our beds… for we have nothing to resist them but one gun with a broken carriage and four muskets, which we bought at our own cost and charges.
(July 1673 petition of Sheringham citizens to the government because of the fear of a Dutch invasion).

There are really two Sheringhams, Upper and Lower. Upper Sheringham was the original village a mile or so inland from the coast with the honour of a mention in William the Conqueror's Domesday Book. Its Domesday form was Silingham - perhaps the place where Scira's people settled. The Norman lord in the Domesday year of 1086 was William de Schoies, and the village then had more goats than people!

In the church of All Saints, Upper Sheringham, there is a maritime link in its little mermaid. Many years ago the mermaid knocked on the door of the church but was refused entry because she 'wasn't a Christian'. She sneaked inside later on and has been there ever since. Look out for her on the end of one of the pews. In front of the church is a reservoir built as a peace symbol at the end of the Napoleonic Wars. Upper Sheringham is not alone in marking the end rather prematurely 'in the year of peace 1814'.

The little mermaid in Upper Sheringham church.

Upper Sheringham church with the slightly ante-dated peace reservoir .

By Tudor times the little offshoot of Lower Sheringham, or Sheringham Hythe, had already developed a sea-going trade, with 200 fishing boats recorded, and the Victorian total was at least this number. In Victorian times it was a village dominated by the fishing industry, with net lofts and boat-building yards, rope walks and whelk coppers scattered between its flint cottages. Boat building was a tradition in Sheringham and its craftsmen provided boats for other towns. The double-ended, clinker-built boats surely hark back to Viking times!

Gradually with the help of the railway, which arrived in 1887, the fishing village grew into an Edwardian holiday resort, and Upper Sheringham, or 'Upper Town', was left behind. As Sheringham developed from fishing village to smart Edwardian resort, 'posh' hotels and private houses were built. Sheringham still boasts a large number

Sheringham Hall in Upper Sheringham, built as the seat of the Upcher family, was reputedly Humphrey Repton's 'most favourite work'.

of buildings from this period. Those interested should start in the Abbey Road and Hook's Hill Road areas. There is a good vantage point for a fine view over the town at Franklin Hill, off Hook's Hill Road. Sheringham, like Rome, boasts seven hills.

With so many boats going daily to sea, it is not surprising that the town developed a proud lifeboat tradition, and it was the local squires, the Upcher family of Sheringham Hall (situated in Upper Sheringham as it happens) who supported the fishermen's safety by providing two of the first (independent) lifeboats. Sheringham is probably unique in having four of its previous lifeboats still in existence. One of these, the 'Henry Ramey Upcher', is still in its original shed. It is amazing to think of the muscle power needed to row these old boats, when the sails were not sufficient. The old 'cork' life-jackets can still be seen in the shed. Amazingly one of the first lifeboat houses, at the 'Old Hythe', was a mile and a quarter to the west of the town, a long run with heavy leather sea-boots!

Close by at Weybourne was the threatened foreign invasion site (see p.84), but it is unlikely that the old cannon that can still be seen in Gun Street, Sheringham, nor the grant of six muskets and a box of shot, would have done a great deal to save the 'Shannocks' (the name for true-born locals) from marauding Dutchmen.

This fine mansion, called The Dales, now a hotel ,was built by Commodore Douglas King MP in 1910.

GANSEYS

Sheringham has a fine tradition of 'gansey' making, (the name for the particular jerseys worn by fishermen in this area), and traditionally knitted by their wives, although there are few knitters today. They were knitted 'in the round', like a sock, using anything from four to eleven needles of size 14-16, and 3-ply blue wool. The patterns used were sometimes handed down in families and were combinations of designs taken from the sea or the weather: coil o'rope, lightning, hailstones, herring-bones, ladders and net-meshes are examples. They are true works of art.

Above: *Evening light towards Weybourne, with Sheringham's 1930s lifeboat house.*

Right: *Sheringham's town clock was once a water reservoir and is sometimes called 'Mary Pym' after the lady who donated it.*

Far right: *Sheringham's west gangway, with the old 'Henry Ramey Upcher' lifeboat shed at the top, still has a colourful collection of boats — though few in number compared to its past.*

Morris Dancers at the 'Potty Festival', named after Sherringham's 'Lobster Potties', the originators of the event.

One house of a Victorian flint terrace in Beeston Road, Sheringham.

Look carefully as you walk around Sheringham, as evidence of the old fishing village is still to be seen, for example, in the flint cottages. Flint is the local building material for most of the Norfolk coast, masses of pure silica deposited in chalk layers, and in former times readily available for the taking. On the beaches it is rounded and almost graded for size by the tides. Look at Sheringham's flint walls to see how regular these flints can be. Some pebbles are as they were taken from the beach, and others are 'knapped', that is chopped apart to reveal the shiny interior. There were further refinements such as squaring the knapped flint into small blocks, or, especially in the churches or grand houses, setting the flint into another stone, such as limestone. Elaborate patterns could be formed and this was known as 'flushwork'. Around the coast will be seen examples of houses faced with flint fragments or similar fragments inserted into mortar joints for strength or decoration. This latter is called 'galleting'.

Sheringham's beach may be a little hard on the feet for visitors to the town, but for the geologist it is one of the most interesting in the country. Even the amateur enthusiast will be amazed at the variety, apart from the flints. Just occasionally small pieces of amber or jet can be found. Legally, beach stones must not be removed now, as they once were both before and after the last war in their thousands of tons, for use in the 'potteries'. A particular 'blue' variety was ground up for use in the china industry. In former days this 'stone picking' provided a winter income for many locals and the piles of stones awaiting collection would be as high as a house. It was an exceptionally hard back-breaking job for those employed.

Among the famous residents of Sheringham have been Ralph Vaughan Williams who composed here whilst staying for a time at a house called 'Martincross' (then called 'Mainsail Haul') close by the war memorial (a plaque marks the house). The play-wright Patrick Hamilton, of 'Gaslight' fame, also lived in this house, and the explorers Sir Edward Shackleton and Captain Robert Scott both stayed there.

Beeston Regis has a slice of history in its own right with the ruins of a priory dating back to 1216. Its probable founder was Margaret de Cressy. The order of Canons was a small local group known as Peterstone. The ruins are interesting, with quite high walls surviving, largely built of flint. The nave of the church did not have aisles, but there was a chancel, a chapter house, transepts and cloisters.

Traditional clinker-built boats are still found occasionally on Sheringham's beach, but once there were over two hundred.

Beeston Church, a little further eastwards, is quite close to the edge of the cliff. It received a mention in the national papers some decades ago when the rector made financial provision against its eventual loss over the edge of the cliff. It still survives and has an interesting brass to a Tudor seaman and his wife, John and Katherine Deynes, 1527. The seaman has a mariner's whistle, and the lady a pomander.

Grass of Parnassus: this plant is rare in Norfolk but is still found in marshy spots. The beautiful flower smells faintly of honey. It was used for complaints of the liver and an infusion of the leaves was reputed to aid digestion.

BEESTON COMMON SSSI

Commons are areas of opportunity for conservation around the country, and none more so than Beeston Common near Sheringham. Thanks to the work of naturalist-extraordinary Ken Durrant and a small but dedicated team, this remarkable area was pulled back from neglect and invasive gorse. Ken and his team responded to Sheringham Council's request for assistance back in 1983-4 and today the results of two decades of loving care are self evident. It was designated an SSSI in 1961. Together with other Norfolk valley fens it was part of an SAC, an international designation. Of flowering plants, 400 species are recorded each year including round-leaved sundew, butterwort and grass of Parnassus; there are 14 species of orchid including the pyramidal. In the pond, marsh cinquefoil is found. There are 28 species of butterfly including the green hairstreak. The SSSI award in 1996 was for outstanding management, the first in Norfolk. The people of north Norfolk should be proud of this naturalists' paradise.

❶ 'Henry Ramey Upcher' lifeboat-shed at the West Gangway on the Promenade, is certainly worth a visit, as it shows off a fine early 'rowing and sailing' vessel.

❷ Priory Maze and Gardens (01263 822986) is an interesting garden development of 10 acres that has become very popular. It has the Foxgloves Tea Rooms and picnic facilities, and is reached from the main road to Cromer. It is close to Beeston Priory, but the ruins of the priory can be reached by turning left (from the Sheringham direction) before the Maze and following the road round to the right.

❸ Sheringham Museum in Station Rd. (01263 821871) has a fascinating collection, reflecting Sheringham's heritage. Plans are well ahead for two new museums telling the story of Sheringham's fishing and lifeboat histories.

❹ Sheringham Park the Upcher family estate in Upper Sheringham, (01263 821429) is now owned by the National Trust, (parking fee for non-members only). There are spectacular displays of rhododendrons and azaleas in season.

❺ 'The Poppy Line' (01263 820800) runs steam rail trips to Weybourne, or further on to Holt. Check with the station for timetables and visit the museum and shop.

❻ TIC, Station Approach (01263 824329).

❼ Walks: westwards to the Old Hythe and back using the beach one way and the cliff path, abutting the Sheringham Golf Links, the other. The low point at the end is the site of a former lifeboat house, and you will also pass the 1936 lifeboat house at the western end of the promenade. The modern inshore boat is an Atlantic 75; through the woods up to Pretty Corner (start up Common Lane) and either back down Holway Road or return along different woodland paths; Beeston Hill is worth a climb (start from Cliff Road) and you can continue onwards to Beeston Church; town walks: a 'Heritage Trail' leaflet and other walks are available from the Museum or book shops.

❽ Pubs and eating places: Sheringham has a good choice of pubs including the Crown (01263 823213); Two Lifeboats Hotel (01263 822401); The Lobster (01263 822716); Upper Sheringham has the Red Lion (01263 825408), and The Dales Hotel (01263 824555); Pretty Corner Tearooms, (01263 822766) at the top of Holway Road, provide refreshments in a woodland setting.

Beeston Priory dates back to 1216 and is built largely of flint.

Beeston Hill from Beeston Common.

15 – The Runtons

On Thursday 1st instant a girl named Martha Holman of this place went up to the mill with a donkey and cart and was in the act of getting out of the cart when one of the sails of the mill caught her on the head so that she turned completely over in falling and alighted flat on her back. She was taken up by Mr Kemp apparently dead and conveyed home. Mr. Buck of Cromer is attending her, but she lies in a very precarious state.
(*Norfolk News* – 10th November 1860)

West Runton has something to offer from the present day to pre-historic times. The village lies between the sea and part of the Cromer Ridge known as Roman Camp. This area was never a 'Roman Camp'. Although there are no known Roman connections, evidence of early metal smelting has been discovered. The Cromer Ridge is a belt of sand and gravel debris stretching from Cromer to Holt, left behind by melting ice sheets at the end of the last Ice Age about 300,000 years ago. Roman Camp, with its woods and heathland, is managed by the National Trust, and is the highest point in Norfolk at 328 feet above sea level. Those who say there are no hills in Norfolk should take a bicycle ride from Runton to Aylmerton through Roman Camp!

A sunny summer's day brings out the crowds on West Runton's sandy beach.

A splash of colour on the seashore.

West Runton still has a small railway station where the local Women's Institute look after the plants and gardens and once a year they also hold an annual tea-party on the platform. The beach, which has an ample car park, has large areas of sand and, unusually for Norfolk, rock-pools. These are well worth exploring at low tide, but be careful to replace any upturned stones and rocks to ensure the wildlife is not left to dry out.

The geological make-up of the cliffs between West Runton and East Runton has led English Nature to designate the area an SSSI. It has a wealth of interest and is used frequently for teaching purposes. It is an excellent site for fossil collectors and after a stormy day or a high tide, freshly exposed fossils can be found. At the base of the cliffs, 200 metres east of West Runton gap, is the dark, two metre thick layer of the 'Cromer Forest Bed'. It is highly fossiliferous and rich in the remains of plants and trees (seeds, cones, wood and fungi), molluscs (terrestrial and aquatic shells), fish (scales, teeth and bones), amphibians, large and small mammals (bones and teeth).

WEST RUNTON ELEPHANT

The first bones of this beast were revealed in December 1990 at the base of the cliff after a storm. They had lain buried for between 600,000 and 700,000 years under twenty metres of cliff. Retrieval of the whole animal was not launched until January 1992. First to be found were the ribs, jaw, backbone and part of a leg. In 1995 major excavations took place to recover the rest of the skeleton. It was estimated that the elephant stood at a height of four metres and its weight was about ten tons. This made it twice as heavy as a modern African elephant. It was reckoned to be around forty years of age at its death. As dinosaurs were extinct by this time, the elephant was one of the larger beasts on land. The climate was also warmer so East Anglia had monkeys, hyenas, rhinoceros and giant moose.

Unearthing the bones of the West Runton elephant. These are not fossilised.

The Shire Horse Centre provides an informative visit for both young and old.

The fossils are between 425,000 and 700,000 years old. Some fifty metres further east is the site of the famous 'West Runton Elephant'. Previously parts of an old elephant were discovered at Weybourne (Sheringham Museum).

West Runton also boasts a nine-hole golf course and visitors can play on purchasing a day ticket. It is an interesting little course with a road running through it. The first few holes are played on relatively level ground with the latter up and down the hills. Across the village green from the golf course is the Shire Horse Centre. The centre not only shows what the shire horses did on farms and in the towns in years past but it also helps to keep the breeds alive. They have four breeds at the centre, Clydesdale, Suffolk Punch, Percheron and Ardenne. There are regular demonstrations of ploughing, drilling, harrowing and the different shoeing techniques used. There is also a museum of horse-drawn farm equipment as well as urban vehicles. There are a number of gypsy and showmen's caravans also on display. For the children there is a collection of small farm animals.

Left: *Rock-pools are relatively uncommon on the Norfolk coast, but provide endless fascination for children and adults – watch out for the crabs!*

Below left: *East Runton looking towards Cromer.*

Below right: *Two impressive railway viaducts cross the road in East Runton.*

FELBRIGG HALL

Felbrigg Hall stands in its own park-land about three miles inland from West Runton. The current house dates from 1621 and was commissioned by Thomas Windham and built by the master-mason Robert Lyminge. The Windham family, wealthy merchants from the town of Wymondham, had held the estate for two hundred years. The west wing was added in the late 17th century. The collection of books in the library was started by William Windham II whose son was a friend of Dr Johnson. The property has the feel of a 'lived–in' house rather than that of a stately home. It was bequeathed to the National Trust by Robert Wyndham Ketton-Cremer in 1969. Felbrigg Great Wood is an SSSI.

Historic Felbrigg Hall.

East Runton is situated between West Runton and Cromer. It is a small village of old Norfolk cottages straggling along the coast road and also spreading inland around the common land with its two ponds. There was a working windmill here built in about 1836. The sails drove three pairs of stones. It is now in private hands and the mill has had a new cap and fantail but has no sails at present.

A feature of the village which is unusual for Norfolk is its two railway viaducts. The village, however, does not have a railway station, but the area was served by two railway companies, the M & GN and the G.E.

THINGS TO DO

❶ Explore the seashore with its rock-pools, sand and cliffs to find the marine life and possibly a fossil or two.

❷ Shire Horse Centre at West Runton: demonstrations with working horses; also Children's Farm, Countryside Collection and Riding Stables; refreshments available (01263 837339). Well signposted.

❸ Walks: along the beach to Cromer; or follow the Norfolk Coast Path inland, a pleasant walk partly through woodland; explore the many lanes and paths at Roman Camp (NT): a cliff top walk from East Runton to West Runton and back along the beach.

❹ Pubs and eating places: The Fishing Boat (01263 515323); and Constantia Cottage restaurant (01263 512017) (Greek with live music) at East Runton. Dormy House Hotel (01263 837537), Mirabelle Restaurant (01263 837396), The Links Country Park Hotel & Golf Club (01263 838383), The Village Inn (01263 838000), all at West Runton.

❺ 'Worth a detour': historic Felbrigg Hall, 17th and 18th century country house with superb walled garden and good walks in the parkland and around the lake. National Trust (01263 837444).

16 – Cromer

There was an old person of Cromer,
Who stood on one leg to read Homer,
When he found he grew stiff
He jumped over the cliff
Which concluded that person of Cromer.
(Edward Lear)

It is strange to think that Cromer started life more as an inland village than a coastal one! Such is the power of the North Sea along this coast, that it can reduce villages to nothing. So it was that Cromer's neighbouring village of Shipden (Shipden-Juxta-Mare) a thriving medieval port with a jetty, suffered such a fate, and the village of Cromer ('Shipden-Juxta-Felbrigg') three-quarters of a mile inland, had to take on a coastal role. Shipden was mentioned in Domesday but Cromer wasn't. There were two churches, one on the edge of the medieval shoreline and one, an earlier building, on the site of the present church. When the coastal church disappeared under the sea, a large rock called 'Church Rock' remained, marking the spot. In the summer of 1888 a paddle steamer 'The Victoria' with passengers from Yarmouth, struck the rock and finally sank. Fortunately no one was lost, but the rock was afterwards demolished. Legends of ghostly bells ringing, as elsewhere along the coast, were probably circulated to keep away any prying eyes that might have witnessed the activities of the local smugglers!

The 15th century tower of the church of St Peter & St Paul, claimed to be the highest parish church in Norfolk, dominates the town.

Cromer's landscape and setting is the result of the Ice Age, and the town is tucked under the end of the Cromer Ridge – the 'terminal moraine' left behind by the ice sheet. Cromer even has the distinction of the term 'Cromerian' for a period in Ice Age history. Its setting certainly drew early visitors to the town. It was in 1793 that one John Gurney (the banking family), a widower with 11 children, is said to have chosen Cromer for his holiday, the first of many 'county' families to do so. For example, the Barclays, Hoares and Buxtons soon followed. Cromer was thus established as a holiday centre with a genteel image complete with Bath House. The poet Swinburne visited, as did Sir Henry Irving, Sir Beerbohm and Lady Tree and Sir Squire and Lady Bancroft. Other visitors to the town were Tennyson, Shackleton and Einstein. In 1887 the Empress Elizabeth of

Cromer pier at sunset.

Austria, the wife of Franz Joseph visited, and in 1907 Princess Stephanie, daughter of King Leopold of the Belgians, stayed in Cliff Avenue. That same year Queen Alexandra, together with the ex-King of Greece and the young Prince Philip, stayed at Newhaven Court. This house was built by Locker Lampson and had many famous guests including Oscar Wilde. He stayed at Grove Farm, Felbrigg and wrote 'A Woman of No Importance'.

As a small boy Winston Churchill stayed at Chesterfield Lodge in West Street. Having apparently thrown an inkwell at his nanny and injured the poor lady, he was taken aside by the local doctor and received a beating for the incident! Edward VII stayed locally with Lord Suffield at Gunton Hall and gave Cromer his seal of approval, by bestowing the 'Royal' title on Cromer's Golf Course. The popularity of Cromer, and the area immediately to the east in late Victorian times, was considerably helped by the writings of the journalist Clement Scott (see p.107) and Cromer's popularity was of course enhanced by the coming of the railway. The Great Eastern arrived in 1877 at Cromer High station and the M & G N (the affectionately named 'Muddle and Get Nowhere') opened the Beach station in 1887.

There is still much architectural evidence of Cromer's building period of the Victorian and Edwardian eras, and Cromer had its own architect in George Skipper (1856-1948). Skipper, the designer of the Royal Arcade in Norwich, was responsible for the Town Hall in 1890, the Grand Hotel in 1891, the Metropole in 1893 and redesigning the Hotel de Paris in 1895-6.

The Gangway and Brunswick Terrace. The Gangway's granite sills were laid in 1882, in a 'saw-tooth' style for horses' hooves to grip.

A reminder of former M & G N days

George Skipper's impressive 'Hotel de Paris' was originally a summer residence of Lord Suffield of Gunton Hall, and was 'Skipperized' in 1895-6.

THE LEGEND OF BLACK SHUCK

If you are walking late at night anywhere near the clifftops between Beeston and Overstrand, and you hear an animal's slow padding behind you, don't look round. It may be the legendary Black Shuck, (Anglo-Saxon 'Scucca') the Hound of Odin, the great war-dog of the Norse raiders. Look in the dog's eyes and your fate is sealed! The dog, in its various forms, synonymous with Satan, pads its way across many counties of England. Interestingly, Sir Arthur Conan Doyle heard the legend, it is said, whilst staying with a golfing colleague in Cromer in 1901, just a year or so before 'The Hound of the Baskervilles' was penned. He also stayed at Cromer Hall and was apparently driven by a coachman named Baskerville. The setting of Baskerville Hall is said to have been based upon Cromer Hall.

Dodging the waves

Cromer Hall, reputedly Conan Doyle's model for Baskerville Hall, was built in 1827 and suffered a severe fire in 1829.

Cromer pier with rough sea.

HENRY BLOGG GC, BEM (1876-1954)

Cromer boasts as one of its sons a man whom few would dispute deserves the title of the most remarkable lifeboatman in the long and proud history of the lifeboat service. Henry Blogg, a local fisherman, was decorated more times than any other lifeboatman. He joined the Cromer lifeboat crew in 1894 aged only 18, and on his retirement in 1947 had served for 53 years, 37 as coxswain. It is probably only other holders of that position who can truly relate to the weight of responsibility that period of service carried with it, because during those years as a lifeboatman Blogg went to sea 387 times, and with his fellow crew members during those launches saved an astonishing 873 lives. Not surprisingly Henry Blogg won the RNLI's Gold medal for gallantry on three occasions, and its Silver on another four, and also the George Cross and British Empire Medal. One such remarkable rescue was that of the SS 'Fernebo', in January 1917, when Blogg and his crew had already had one 'shout' that day. The lifeboat 'Louisa Heartwell' was a rowing and sailing boat and the average age of the crew was 50. They had faced the North Sea for 14 hours. In another spectacular rescue in 1933 Blogg drove his lifeboat twice, right on to the deck of the barge 'Sepoy', to scoop up two crew members. In private this remarkable man is remembered as quite shy and immeasurably modest about his achievements. Henry Blogg's career is fittingly marked in the 'Henry Blogg Museum' (see 'Things to do').

Cromer Hall was built in 1827 for the Wyndham family, and is impressively Gothick in its grey flintwork. It suffered a fire shortly after it was built. The original architect was Donthorne. The hall has 'Sherlock Holmes' connections (see p100).

The present church is a magnificent 15th century building well worth exploring. It is dedicated to St Peter and St Paul as a link with the former church of Shipden. It was rebuilt from a previous one which had fallen into a state of disrepair. Even so in 1683 the chancel had again fallen into a sorry state and was blown up! There was also major renovation work in the later Victorian period. The tower is an amazing 160 feet high and it is not surprising that this served as an early lighthouse.

The present pier was opened in 1901, the old jetty having been damaged in 1897 by a cargo ship. In July 1940 it was cut in half to prevent its use by invading forces. It was claimed someone had forgotten the necessary access to the lifeboat on the end of the pier, so the gap had to be bridged! It suffered serious damage in 1993 when a barge cut loose from its moorings and crashed through the pier, but it reopened the following year. The RNLI shed was replaced by a larger building in 1998. In its very popular Pavilion Theatre, Cromer claims to have the last traditional 'end of pier' show.

The Cromer Lighthouse built in 1832 which replaced the coal-fired 1719 building.

Cromer's first lighthouse was built in 1719 ; the present lighthouse, with its octagonal tower, was built in 1832. It has proved of great value for those navigating the seas off Cromer – sometimes called the 'Devil's Throat'.

❶ Cromer Hall is a short walk from the Methodist Church up Hall Road. It is not open to the public but can easily be seen from the road.

❷ Cromer Museum (01263 513543): old fishermen's cottages (reopens 2006 season: including the Poppyland story and Norfolk geology).

❸ Railway buffs, will still find evidence of the former (M & GN) Beach Station buildings (now a pub). The Marriot signal box (viewable from the station platform) is of interest.

❹ The Pier is open all the year and has a lively theatre, 'The Pavilion', (01263 512495) with a regular summer show.

❺ Lifeboat: the current lifeboat can be visited at the end of the pier.

❻ The RNLI Henry Blogg Museum, (01263 511294) is situated on the promenade at the bottom of the Gangway. The Museum tells the story of Cromer's lifeboats and of the most remarkable lifeboatman ever.

❼ TIC Bus Station, Prince of Wales Road (01263 512497).

❽ Walks: to the lighthouse from the promenade along the cliff-top, passing through the area known as 'Happy Valley'. A road-based return can be taken if preferred, down the hill to the coast road. For the possibility of lighthouse visits check with TIC; from Cromer to East Runton along the beach (checking on tides). The walk can be continued from East Runton to West Runton; 'A Cromer Walk' leaflet is available from TIC (worth it for the illustrations); Cromer Church and Chapel Trail (leaflet from the TIC).

❾ Pubs and eating places: 'Buffers' (01263 514000), old M & G N station; the Red Lion (01263 514964); Hotel de Paris (01263 513141); White Horse Inn (01263 512275); Tides Restaurant, on the pier (01263 511236) also Pier Pavilion foyer bar; Albion Hotel, (01263 513135); Wellington Hotel, (01263 511075); King's Head, (01263 512296).

Cromer from the air.

A view from the lighthouse across Happy Valley.

17 – Overstrand

The peaceful stillness of an English summer after-noon brooded over the park and gardens at Overdene.
A hush of moving sunlight and lengthening shadows lay upon the lawn, and a promise of
refreshing coolness made the shade of the great cedar tree a place to be desired.
(from *The Rosary* by Florence Barclay, 1862 – 1921, Overstrand author)

Overstrand was originally a crab-fishing village; the fishing still continues but on a much smaller scale. The fine sandy beaches below the cliff are clean and safe. The village came to prominence in the late 19th century when the Victorian pastime of sea-bathing came into fashion. The village was made popular at this time by Clement Scott, a journalist with the Daily Telegraph and the Morning Post (see next chapter). The village became known as the 'Village of the Millionaires' because it was visited by the rich and famous, many of whom built second homes here. Winston Churchill stayed here during the First World War and is said to have mobilised the British fleet from the telephone of a mansion called 'Sea Marge'. Churchill's father owned a house in the village called 'Pear Tree Cottage'. Other famous and regular visitors to the village were the Prince of Wales, the Duke of Marlborough and Albert Einstein .

Alexanders was introduced as a vegetable by the Romans and is very prolific along roadsides near the coast.

On walking around the village one can see the influence of its past wealthy residents. There are a number of buildings which are not typical of a Norfolk village, such as the 'multi-listed' house called 'The Pleasaunce'. 'The Pleasaunce', was built in 1897-99 from a design by Sir Edwin Lutyens, for Lord and Lady Battersea, the latter a member of the Rothschild family. The grounds and gardens were designed jointly by Gertrude Jekyll and Lutyens, who worked together on a number of projects. The building contains aspects of many styles from Classical to 'Arts and Crafts', and notable external features are the stable yard clock tower and the covered walkway, which ends in an octagonal summer house. The sumptuous rooms were once filled with 'Arts and Crafts' furniture along with Pre-Raphaelite works of art. Some rooms, such as the dining room, have oak panelling, and many of the fireplaces are decorated with De Morgan tiles. The relationship between the clients and the architect was often a stormy one, and Lady Battersea it is said, even resorted to hurling bricks from the balcony outside her bedroom because

The cormorant dives for food and nests on cliff ledges.

An interesting Lutyens building in Overstrand is the Methodist Church.

she considered it too high. 'The Pleasaunce' is not open to the public and it now operates as a holiday home managed by the Federation of Christian Endeavour Holiday Homes Ltd. The Batterseas also commissioned Lutyens to design the Methodist Church in Overstrand and this is thought to be the only non-conformist church he designed. It has a brick lower floor with a pebble-dash and glass clerestory above.

Overstrand Hall is another of the village's extravagant mansions, designed by Lutyens for Lord and Lady Hillingdon. It is now an activity centre for young people. The splendid mock-Tudor 'Sea Marge', now a hotel and restaurant, was designed by Arthur Blomfield for Sir Edgar Speyer. Sir Edgar, a friend of Elgar, was a banker who helped to fund the London Underground. During the First World War he was deported because he had German connections.

'Sea Marge', is a fine mock-tudor mansion built for the banker Sir Edgar Speyer.

The Pleasaunce' was designed by Lutyens in co-operation with Gertrude Jekyll who designed the gardens.

The White Horse.

105

SIR EDWIN LANDSEER LUTYENS (1869-1944)

Born in 1869, Lutyens studied architecture in London before setting up his own practice in 1888. He was to design many English country houses, his first commission being a private house at Crooksbury, Surrey. It was here that he met Gertrude Jekyll, the garden designer, and the two of them worked together on many designs. He married Emily Lytton in 1897 and they had five children. His initial designs were in the Arts & Crafts style but in the early 1900s his work became more classical in style. He worked on India's fine capital of New Delhi. After the Great War he designed the Cenotaph in London, the Memorial to the Missing of the Somme and the War Memorial Gardens in Dublin. In 1929 he was commissioned to design a new Roman Catholic Cathedral in Liverpool but World War II and a lack of funds only saw the crypt built initially. This was later finished in 1967. Lutyens died in 1944.

Like many of the villages along this stretch of the Norfolk coast, Overstrand is especially vulnerable to encroachment from the sea. As the cliffs erode so they reveal their contents such as fossils. Some of the finds here have included parts of red deer, musk ox and weasel, showing that these animals have been around for a long time. The weasel fossil for example, is part of a leg bone and is about one million years old. Have a look at the base of the cliffs and see what you can find but a word of warning, the cliffs are fragile and unstable so do not climb on them and stick to the specified paths.

The sandy cliffs are being eroded at an alarming rate and new roadways have rapidly disappeared. The Sea Marge Hotel, for example, once well inland, now finds its garden is virtually on the cliff edge and much of the village is in danger. A particular problem here relates to the nature of the cliff material and its drainage. Cliff falls ('slumps') are common. Not surprisingly a residents' action group is fighting for the village's survival, particularly if a policy decision is taken to do nothing further to defend this coast.

THINGS TO DO

❶ **Visit:** St Martin's church which is situated at the end of the village on the Cromer road. Originally built in the Middle Ages it was restored in 1914.

❷ **Walk:** a circular walk over rolling countryside which takes in Northrepps and Southrepps. It is waymarked all the way and is a walk of about 8 miles. There are pubs 'en route'! Walk round the village: most of the interesting architecture in Overstrand is viewable from the roads and alleyways and will reward a pleasant stroll.

❸ **Pubs and eating places:** Sea Marge Hotel (01263 579579), mock-tudor building; sea views from garden; The White Horse, (01263 579237); Cliff Top Café (01263 579319).

A maze of crabpots, stacked ready for use.

18 – Sidestrand and Trimingham

It was one of those farmhouses that is an exact representation of the style of cottage that all children are set to draw when they commence their first lesson. A little red-brick house with three white windows on the first floor, a little white door in the middle, a window at either side and a stack of chimneys at each end of the cottage.
(Clement Scott)

Such is the power of the press that when the Daily Telegraph sent its theatre critic Clement Scott to report on the progress of a new rail link to Cromer, that reporter's love affair with the area between Cromer and Trimingham affected the immediate future of tourism here. From the smoke and smogs of London Town, Clement Scott discovered an idyllic location in Sidestrand and he was prepared to share this rural paradise with the world at large. He coined the term 'Poppyland' for an area where the wild red poppies grew in profusion, and so popularized this corner of Norfolk that the rich and the famous soon discovered it as well. The poet Swinburne visited and wrote 'Songs before Sunrise' whilst staying in Sidestrand.

Clement Scott's Mill House became his ideal rural retreat.

At Sidestrand, Scott discovered a ruined church tower on the edge of the cliff, and the remains of the graveyard which he described as the 'garden of sleep'. At the Mill House, he stayed with Miller Jermy and was looked after by his daughter Louie whom Scott christened 'the Maid of the Mill'.

Scott's writing was sentimental, but of its period, and it had an enormous impact on the whole area. The GER capitalized on Scott's success and produced many railway posters encouraging people to use their trains to discover Scott's idyll for themselves. Louie Jermy's life was also changed by Scott's chance discovery of The Mill House, and achieved a kind of fame through his writing. She spent some time in London and was in service briefly to the family of the artist Sir Edward Burne-Jones. In 1916, shortly after the death of Miller Jermy, Scott's old tower fell over the cliff.

Winter light on Sidestrand's round and octagonal-towered church.

The age of the original Sidestrand church of St Michael and All Angels is in doubt, but there were 14th and 15th century changes to it. Its tower, part round and part octagonal, had stood until 1841 when it is said to have fallen on a stormy night. James

Sidestrand Hall the home of the Hoare family is now a school.

Farm with 'golf ball.'

Craske, an Overstrand bricklayer was given the task of re-building it, and this he completed in 1848. His round tower, however, barely reached the height of the nave. In 1880 the church was moved inland stone by stone and rebuilt (with the financial assistance of Sir Samuel Hoare III and others) in its original form, a third of a mile inland. It was re-consecrated in 1881. A new tower was added to this re-built church, more in keeping with the original, and Craske's tower was the one Clement Scott discovered on the edge of the cliff. Interestingly the tower at Sidestrand was 'moved around' the coast by post-card manufacturers! The Poppyland theme became a growth industry with books, glassware and china being produced. Daniel Davies, a Cromer chemist and photographer, produced 'Poppyland Bouquet' as perfume and soap, and this sold world-wide.

The cliffs along this coast reach their spectacular highest point at Beacon Hill Trimingham at 224 feet, but as elsewhere are gradually being eroded and must be treated with great caution. During the war time Trimingham beach was heavily mined and remained inaccessible for many years after the end of the war.

As well as breeding in Norfolk the meadow pipit is an abundant passage migrant and also winter visitor to the fresh water marshes, sand dunes and grassy banks of our coast.

Looking towards Trimingham from the west.

Knapped and squared flints are a feature of several of the houses in Trimingham. The chips of flint set into the marker (for strength or decoration) are called 'galletting'.

Trimingham Church (13th and 14th centuries) is dedicated to 'The Head of John the Baptist' probably the only one in the country so dedicated. The head is said to have been brought here from Judaea, but may well have been simply a copy in alabaster. Nevertheless the church was reputedly the site of miracles associated with this. Inside Trimingham Church are many fine carvings by a former rector, Revd. Reginald Charles Page, including a peace memorial panel. This depicts a scene of trench warfare with an officer and his men repelling an attack and an aeroplane overhead. There are old 'poppy-head' bench ends, including two by Page, and a 15th century screen, with some original colour.

A very strange modern addition just outside Trimingham village is the giant 'golfball'. It is situated on the site of the original Trimingham radar masts. The 'golf ball' was added to provide protection for the radar equipment.

The wild red poppies are once again seen in abundance in Norfolk's fields, a reminder of Clement Scott's 'poppy land'.

THINGS TO DO

❶ **Sidestrand Churchyard** has the grave of Louie Jermy 'The Maid of the Mill'.

❷ **'The Mill House'** (not open to the public) is now just east of the village of Overstrand and can be seen from the road. The boundary between Overstrand and Sidestrand was changed in 1906.

❸ **Trimingham Church** has a thatched lych-gate and interesting carving.

❹ **Walks:** Clement Scott's 'garden of sleep' (approximate site allowing for erosion) can be found by turning off the main coast road along Tower Lane; Trimingham cliffs: a path leads across a field and through a small wood just as you enter the village from the west. An approach may be made to the cliffs but the descent to beach level is difficult. Take great care!

❺ **Pubs:** Woodlands Caravan Site (licensed); see also Overstrand and Mundesley.

19 – Mundesley and Paston

Whosoever should dwell at Paston should have need to know how to defend himself.
(John Paston, after he had placed his sons to study in the Inns of Court)

The village of Mundesley has largely grown up on either side of the coast road; this runs along the cliff top before turning sharply inland after crossing the mill stream, the River Mun. The village name means 'the woodland clearing with the muddy pool'. No doubt the pool was where the old mill now is, at the point where the stream tumbles down the cliff to the shore. It came into importance during the nineteenth century with the coming of the railway and the Victorians' passion for sea-bathing and 'taking the air'. This stretch of coast from Mundesley west to Sheringham became a mecca for Victorian holidaymakers. The Hotel Continental (formerly the Grand Hotel), is now very dilapidated; and no longer a hotel, although shades of its former glory can still be seen. It overlooks the sea near the church and was once the height of luxury. It was only a short distance from the Midland and Great Northern station which boasted platforms, each 600 feet long, built to accommodate the excursion trains from London, the midlands and the north. Later on, still satisfying the carefree needs of visitors to the area, camping coaches were introduced at the station. This was the railway companies' answer to self-catering holidays. The disappearance of the railway and the station followed Dr. Beeching's 'axe' in the 1960s.

The Manor Hotel and the bomb disposal team Memorial.

Mundesley is still a holiday village. It has fine sandy beaches below the cliffs and good walks in the area. Local clubs and societies arrange special shows and exhibitions with the tourist population in mind.

The poet William Cowper spent some time in the village towards the end of his life staying in a house, 33 High Street, now called Cowper House.

The parish church of All Saints stands proudly on the cliff top. One notices immediately the absence of a tower. The tithe map of 1839 shows the church about one hundred yards from the cliff; now it is about forty yards from the edge. In the 1950s the Rector, Revd John Gedge, persuaded the authorities to extend the promenade westwards, thus

Timeless pleasures of play on the beach.

Cowper House, 33 High Street.

Stow Mill on the Paston road out of Mundesley.

112

protecting the foot of the cliff and the church. The church was a virtual ruin up until the beginning of the 20th century when restoration was completed.

The beach as elsewhere on this stretch of the coast is cleaned regularly and dogs are banned from May until September. Lifeguards are in attendance so safety is paramount for those who wish to swim in the sea or play in the pools left by the receding tide.

Whilst never a port as such, small boats did trade from here. They were run up the beach at high tide and then floated off again at subsequent high tides. They brought in cargoes of coal and shipped out grain.

After leaving Mundesley, you pass a windmill known as Stow Mill. It was built in 1825-27 for James Gaze and it remained in the Gaze family until 1906. It worked as a mill until 1930 when it was bought and converted to living accommodation. In 1938 it was sold to Douglas McDougall, the flour-producing magnate, who used it as a holiday home. In 1999 it was sold to the present owners who have restored it to full working order as a tourist attraction.

The small village of Paston, further along the coast road, is named after the Paston family who lived here in the late medieval and Tudor periods. They were yeoman farmers who raised their status by becoming lawyers. Margaret Paston was the matriarch of the family and lived during the fifteenth century. As the men in such families were so often away from home, the running of the home and estates was left to their wives. Margaret was a formidable woman and as such was often the driving force within the family. It was she who directed the course of her children's lives so that they should have more influence in the county's and the nation's affairs. At Paston the Great Barn can be seen which was built in 1580 by the family; it measures 160 feet long by 60 feet high. The Wodehouse barn at Waxham is similar (see p125); local rivalry perhaps. The family was also responsible for founding a Grammar School at North Walsham (1606) where Lord Nelson was educated for a time.

Mundesley museum, reputedly the smallest in Britain.

THE PASTON LETTERS

Between the years of 1422 and 1509 a series of letters was written, mostly by Margaret Paston, which give a remarkable insight into the life of the period. These letters were mainly addressed to her husband, a lawyer who lived in London for most of his time. Some contain 'family gossip' whilst others seek advice. The ownership of property or land could still be a precarious business at that time. Often the content of the letters contain pleas for her husband to return to Norfolk and sort out situations where the Paston property was in danger of being possessed by others. In the 18th century William Paston, 2nd Earl of Yarmouth sold the letters and some of them were published. The originals disappeared but were found in the mid 19th century and are now in the British Museum.

❶ All Saints church: stands on the clifftop. Much restored from a virtual ruin, at the beginning of the 20th century.

❷ John of Gaunt's house, Gimingham: John of Gaunt, one of the largest landowners in England, owned the manor of Gimingham. This house, dating from circa 1560, probably stands on the site of an earlier wooden house occupied by one of John of Gaunt's bailiffs.

❸ Mundesley Maritime Museum (01263 720879): small museum in the former Coastguard lookout. Exhibits about the lifeboat, coastguards, the railway and minefields.

❹ Mundesley Visitor and Advice Centre, Station Rd (01263 721070).

❺ Paston Great Barn: Tudor barn. Information from English Nature (01733 455190).

❻ St Margaret's Church, Paston; this has some wall paintings.

❼ Stow Mill, (01263 720298) demonstration of how a mill works.

❽ Pubs and eating places: Royal Hotel (01263 720096) has Nelson memorabilia; Manor Hotel (01263 720309); Ship Inn, (01263 720448); Tea Caddy Tea Rooms, (01263 721751).

Above: *John of Gaunt House.*
Left: *The magnificent Paston barn built in 1580.*

20 – Bacton and Walcott

But wenden to Walsingham and my wife Alis, and byd the Roode of Bromholme bring me out of dette.
(Piers Plowman)

Bacton has been a settlement since Anglo-Saxon times when the village was called Bectuna (Bec's town). William the Conqueror gave the manor to one of his principal barons, Robert Mallet, who subsequently gave it to one of his followers, Robert de Glanville. The 15th century church of St Andrew is situated a little way from the main village. This usually indicates that the Black Death hit the village hard and afterwards the village was rebuilt on a new site. The church, being the only stone building, stayed in its old position. The Great Plague of the 17th century also ravaged the village. There is a fine sandy beach with safe bathing.

Robert de Glanville's son, William, founded Bromholme Priory as a house of Cluniac monks subordinate to Castle Acre Priory. Originally there were only seven or eight monks. The fortunes of the abbey changed in 1233 when it purchased a fragment of the 'true' cross which had been rescued earlier by St Helen, mother of Constantine the Great. The Bromholme fragment was special because it was said to have been 'most besprinkled by Christ's blood'. The fortunes and wealth of the priory increased as 'miracles' happened. The blind regained their sight, cripples were healed and even the dead were brought back to life by means of the relic. Important people visited the priory along with many pilgrims. In 1233, Henry III resided here with his court for a time. By 1291 the priory had rents in 56 parishes in Norfolk and Norwich. In 1313 Edward II visited and granted the priory the manor of Bacton. The Pastons were also great patrons. The funeral of Sir John Paston took place in the priory church in 1466 and many people came. The church had to be evacuated as so many candles were lit, the building filled with smoke and it was hard to breathe! At the dissolution of the monasteries the lands of Bromholme were given to the Wodehouse family of Waxham.

In the mid-1960s a natural gas terminal was built at Bacton, this being the closest point to the North Sea gas fields. For many years most of Britain's gas entered here. The principal operator is Shell, with Transco being the distributor.

The gatehouse, Bromholme Priory, Bacton.

Bacton gas terminal where the nation's gas enters the mainland.

Walcott is a quiet seaside village with a fine beach below the sea wall. It is often bypassed except by caravanners in the summer months. Sea defences here are made of concrete which give a 'promenade' feel to the place. The 15th century church of All Saints is away from the village sitting rather bleakly in the surrounding fields. It contains an art deco lectern and organ. The font is 13th century, from an earlier church, and is of Purbeck marble. There is a fine piscina (for washing communion vessels) together with a sedilia (the priest's seat) in the chancel.

THINGS TO DO

❶ Bacton church of St Andrew is to the west of the village. Built in the mid 15th century it has a fine carved font.

❷ Bromholme Priory (sometimes known as Broomholm): visit the Gate-house. You can see the ruins, on private property, in the fields by the farm.

❸ Walcott church of All Saints stands alone by the coast road. It has some art-deco pieces inside and a piscina and sedilia in the chancel.

❹ Walk; Bacton Wood, contact North Norfolk District Council (01263 513811).

❺ Pubs and eating places; Poacher's Pocket, (01692 650467); The Light-house, (01692 650371); Seaview Café, (01692 650283); The Duke of Edinburgh, (01692 650280); Ship Inn, (01692 650420).

Walcott promenade and beach in early spring.

Walcott's ancient church in a sea of narcissi.

Walcott to Winterton-on-Sea

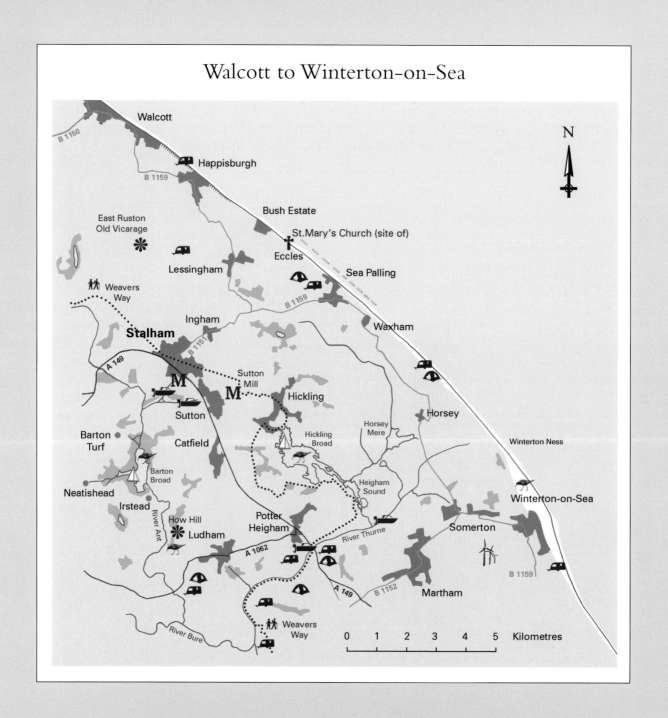

21 – Happisburgh and Eccles

As singular a countryside as any in England, where a few scattered cottages represented the population
of today, while on every hand enormous square-towered churches bristled up from the flat, green
landscape and told of the glory and prosperity of old East Anglia.
(Conan Doyle, *The Dancing Men*, written in Happisburgh.)

Norfolk names are a test for keen spellers and Happisburgh (pronounced 'Haisbro') is no exception! It possibly derives from the Old English personal name Haep, and gets a mention in Domesday. Happisburgh has a long maritime history – both within and outside the law; it has a church that, like the lighthouse, has provided a beacon for ships, and a pub where the landlord had the right of wreck along the foreshore – and probably still has.

The tall red-and-white painted lighthouse, built in 1790 (once a painting challenge for Anneka Rice's team in the TV series) is a reflection of just how treacherous this particular section of Norfolk coast has been to shipping. It was orignally one of a pair. In 1990 the lighthouse was saved as a private trust, and now operates as the only independent lighthouse in the country. Off-shore are the dangerous 'Haisbro Sands' and onshore there have been repeated inroads of the sea over the centuries. The battle is still being fought.

To the seaward side was a village called Wimpwell under the control of the Abbot of St Benets (on the Broads). Wimpwell was a very early Christian settlement – a fishing village in Saxon times – but it almost disappeared overnight in January 1604, with 1000 acres of land it was said. Eccles was to suffer the same fate and the present village is a shadow of its former self.

St Mary's church Happisburgh once belonged to the monks of Wymondham Abbey (another Norfolk spelling – pronounced 'Windham'). Its graveyard unfortunately reflects the loss of life to the sea. There was for example in 1770 the wreck of *HMS Peggy*, an eight-gun naval sloop used against smugglers in the North Sea. It ran ashore on Happisburgh beach near the Town Gap. There were 52 survivors, but a further 32 lost their lives. A similar tragedy was that of the *Invincible*, a 74-gun ship that was about

Between autumn and spring the purple sandpiper visits us from Greenland and Scandinavia.

WILLIAM COWPER (1731-1800)

The poet William Cowper visited Happisburgh with his cousin Revd. Dr John Johnson who would rent a house at Mundesley for a holiday. The latter wrote in 1798: 'I coaxed him (Cowper) into a boat in which he and I and our servant were rowed to Happisburgh. He went with me to see the lighthouse and appeared to enjoy in some measure looking thro' a telescope from that very lofty building, at the ships in the offing. After dining at the Public House on the Hill, we walked home – the sea being too rough for us to return in the boat.' That walk would have been about five miles.

Thrift is equally at home in the very different coastal habitats of cliff tops and saltmarshes.

to join the Baltic fleet where Nelson was second-in-command. They had left Yarmouth Roads under a young captain John Rennie when they struck a sandbank off Happisburgh and went down. A huge grave was dug near the church and 119 (of the 400 lost) sailors buried. It was as late as 1998 that a simple memorial stone was at last unveiled in the churchyard to the sailors who died.

The strangest of all the burials seen here was probably that of a poisoner, Jonathan Balls, who in 1846 was buried with a plum cake, a bible, a poker and a pair of tongs, which still remain a mystery. It was suspected he may have accidentally succumbed to a lethal dose of his own poison!

As with any fishing community the benefit of wreck, when it unfortunately happened, was one to be taken advantage of in terms of what was washed up on the beaches. When barrels of brandy appeared along the shore intact, the bonus was very tangible, but equally there might be barrels of flour, candles, pit-props or bales of material, depending upon the cargo of the unfortunate ship. When a collier foundered the coal-sheds of the local communities would be supplied for months.

The 'public house on the hill' of Cowper's time, 'Hill House' goes back to the 16th century and was earlier known as the 'Windmill Inn'. In addition to Cowper, a further

SMUGGLING

The Hill House pub Happisburgh, where Sir Arthur Conan Doyle stayed.

It would seem that smuggling was a national pastime. Dutch gin (Geneva), brandy, tea and tobacco were favourites with the 'gentlemen'. Hill House in Happisburgh had a strong smuggling tradition as did the Lifeboat Inn at Thornham. There were various roads near Bacton used by smugglers and at Weybourne deep water off shore allowed large vessels to lay close by. Brancaster Staithe's most famous smuggler was William Hotching. He used his smuggling to stock his own beer-house, 'The Hat and Feather'. His cutter, *The Harlequin* would meet Dutch boats at sea. At Stiffkey they would cover cartloads of smuggled goods with seaweed. In Wells the linked attics in some of the terraces assisted smugglers' escape. At Kelling Hard smugglers would bury themselves under the beach stones and rise up to petrify any watching strangers. The romanticised view of smugglers was often far from the truth however. In Old Hunstanton churchyard are the graves of a Customs Officer and a soldier of the 15th Light Dragoons both killed by smugglers.

literary connection is with Sir Arthur Conan Doyle who stayed at Hill House and wrote a Sherlock Holmes story here, entitled 'The Adventure of the Dancing Men'. It is said that the 'dancing men' code used in the story (matchstick men) was picked up from watching the landlord's son, Gilbert Cubitt, playing with these. The boy's surname was used in the story.

The village's largest private house is St Mary's built for the Cater family in 1900 by the architect Detmar Blow, a follower of William Morris. He used traditional flint and thatch, and the design is in the shape of a butterfly'. It is a very fine house and Blow was highly regarded in his time. Worryingly the house is now within sight of a watery grave. Local action groups have been formed to defend Happisburgh against the sea as many of its properties are at risk from the rapid erosion of the cliffs.

An unusual, nautical garden in Eccles. Mrs Beryl Kerrison raises money for lifeboat work from her many visitors. She and her late husband Sam collected flotsam and jetsam.

Eccles-Juxta-Mare was in medieval times a flourishing fishing village covering some 2000 acres. The name almost certainly seems to be derived from the Latin word for church, 'ecclesia'. After the destruction of the village in the 17th century, the church tower, 'The Lonely Sentinel', stood isolated on the beach. In January 1895 a great storm finally demolished the remains of the church. The outline of the original town occasionally re-appears after a tidal 'scour', as in 1986 and 1991, with traces of the old towers' stone foundations. Also old ships' timbers sometimes appear from long-dead colliers that plied this coast. Archaeological finds such as Roman pottery, medieval buckles and pilgrims' badges have been recorded.

From the 14th century the local lord of the manor was entitled to one hundred herrings for each fishing boat's crew 'washing their nets' at Eccles, giving an indication of the fishing trade here, plus an even more unusual perk known as 'bedgeld'. This was the right to 'consummate the nuptials of the bride', unless commuted to a fee!

Today masonry on the beach together with a few bungalows and beach chalets are all that remain of this once important village. In the 1930s there had been a move to re-create something of its former scale, with a planned 700-plus bungalows, but World War II intervened before the entire development was carried out.

❶ **The Church of St Mary's** Happisburgh has one of the finest towers in Norfolk at 110 feet high – even though it is not in alignment with the rest of the building! Tower tours are available regularly throughout the year for hardy climbers.

❷ **The lighthouse** is now operated by the independent Happisburgh Lighthouse Trust. It is open to the public on limited occasions throughout the year.

❸ **Walk** along Beach Road and find a vantage point to view the superb flint design of 'St Mary's', not easy to miss. Further along, steps lead down to the beach with an excellent panorama eastwards towards Sea Palling. For drivers, there is a small car-park near the steps.

❹ **Pubs:** Hill House (01692 650004) is worth a visit for its refreshments and for those interested in the Sherlock Holmes connection. The pub has memorabilia of Sir Arthur Conan Doyle's visit and especially of course linked to 'The Adventure of the Dancing Men' story.

❺ **'Worth a detour':** The Swan at Ingham, (01692 581099); East Ruston Old Vicarage Gardens, (01692 650432), fascinating development on an open site.

St Mary's is a fine flint and thatch building designed in 1900 by the architect Detmar Blow.

Happisburgh lighthouse is a striking landmark from land and sea. It is now privately maintained.

22 – Sea Palling, Waxham and Horsey

The waters, which were up to two metres higher than normal, hit just after six o'clock on the evening of Saturday 31st January. Norfolk's badly neglected sea defences didn't stand a chance.
(*Eastern Daily Press* 2nd February 1953.)

Sea Palling is a small village which straggles along the coast road and down the road which leads to the beach. The houses are mostly modern in construction. There has been a settlement here for many centuries. The old church of St Margaret has features dating from the 14th and 15th centuries. Inside the church the Sea Palling Lifeboat Commemoration Boards can be viewed, and there is still an inshore lifeboat at Sea Palling today. The village sign depicts the lifeboat being launched in a rough sea. It is one of some 200 carved by the late Harry Carter, art and craft master at Hamond's Grammar School, Swaffham.

In the 18th and 19th centuries smuggling was rife along the Norfolk coast and Sea Palling did its share. Cargoes of tea, tobacco and spirits were often 'washed up' on Palling beach. It continued despite the efforts of the Excise patrol from Happisburgh who had the support of the local dragoon guards. In 1777 a large quantity of spirits was seized between Palling and Waxham.

In the mid 1990s the Environment Agency funded a beach reclamation and sea defence scheme. They constructed reefs off the shore which have maintained sand deposits on the beach. After these changes the beach now has miles of golden sand. The area is designated as an AONB and in 2003 Sea Palling beach was awarded Blue Flag Status, the European safe beach standard. A bank of dunes planted with marram grass (a natural feature along this coast reinforced by man) protects the marsh and the village from high tides although, as elsewhere, in 1953 the sea broke through and the floods caused immense damage and loss of life. During the night people took to their rooftops to escape the water and in all, seven persons were drowned. Sea Palling was crushed.

Waxham today is a small village. In Saxon times there were two villages, Waxham Magna and Waxham Parva, and these existed before the Danish conquest in AD 867. Waxham

Lambs play on the grazing marsh behind the sea-defence bank near Sea Palling.

Sea Palling beach showing offshore reefs and the 'rock armour' now widely used along Norfolk's coast.

A bright spring day on the remote beach at Horsey Gap.

Parva has long since disappeared into the sea. The Domesday Book of 1086 records a church at Waxham Magna. The current church of St John dates mainly from the 14th and 15th centuries. Inside, the 14th century font has an unusual brick pedestal. On the north wall is the 16th century tomb of Thomas Wodehouse, one of the Lords of the Manor.

At Waxham there is a combination of the church, the hall and the barn in one area. On the seaward side the hall has high walls with a large gate which were built in the 15th century. For many years the Lords of the Manor, the Wodehouse family, lived in the hall. The hall is supposed to be haunted by five ghosts, all of them knights and all died in battle! As a symbol of their wealth, the Wodehouse family built a great barn in the 16th century. It has the longest thatched barn roof in the country and is one of the largest farm buildings in Britain. It was almost destroyed in the great gale of 1987 and it has since been restored at a cost of almost half a million pounds.

The tiny village of Horsey stands below sea level and the sea is kept at bay by a huge sand and shingle bank. It is here that the area known as the Broads meets the sea. Horsey windmill was a pump which was used to take water off the marsh and into the dykes. Today this is done by electric pumps. This mill and Horsey Mere are owned by the National Trust. From the dyke by the mill it is possible to sail into the Broads.

The famous Horsey Mill, where the coast meets the Broads.

Waxham barn has the longest thatched barn roof in Britain. Part of the barn complex was built to repel the Spanish Armada invasion.

NORFOLK REEDS

A Norfolk reed-bed.

Reed has been used for thatching for many centuries, probably since man first settled near wetlands. Up until the middle of the 19th century it was the most common material on the roofs of houses in Norfolk. The clay pan-tile was another popular material for roofing. The coming of the railways brought in cheap Welsh slate and so reed thatch became less common. The best reed is grown on marshland which floods, rather than on that which is continually under water. The reed-beds are harvested every two years; this allows the plant to grow to the correct length of about two metres. The reed is harvested from December through to March either by hand or by machine. Either way it is hard, wet and cold work. Some reed cutters will tell you that hand-cut reed is the best. Which ever way it is cut, it should be cut below the water-line as this is where the reed is hardest. This is the end of the reed which is exposed on a roof and therefore needs to be the most durable. About 400 bundles of reed can be cut from one acre of reed-bed. Each bundle will cover the same roof area as a tile.

THINGS TO DO

❶ **Horsey Mill** (01493 393904) is technically a windpump and one of the most photographed 'mills' in Norfolk. The five floors of the windpump afford wonderful views across Horsey Mere and the surrounding countryside. It is run by the National Trust.

❷ **Sea Palling church:** examples of changing building styles from 14th and 15th centuries; 14th century font; Lifeboat Commemorative Boards just inside the door.

❸ **Waxham Barn** built in Tudor times by the Wodehouse family has the longest thatched barn roof in the country, .

❹ **Walk;** waymarked circular walk around Horsey Mere with lovely views; details available from the mill; coastal walks on the dunes or the beach from Horsey Gap.

❺ **Pubs and places to eat;** Old Hall Inn, (01692 598323), Sea Palling: Nelson's Head (01493 393378), Horsey.

23 – Winterton-on-Sea, Hemsby and Scratby

Country people had scarce a barn, or a shed, or a stable – but what was built of old planks, beams, wales and timbers etc, the wrecks of ships and ruins of mariners' and merchants' fortunes.
(Daniel Defoe, passing through the Winterton area)

Winterton-on-Sea (the addition to its name was made as late as the 1950s) was in medieval times a sizeable and important port. But Winterton Ness was thought by many sailors to be one of the most dangerous headlands between the Thames and the Tyne, with numerous wrecks. Ships would have to make certain of clearing the headland by navigating out to sea, often under very difficult conditions. Salvage was at times a profitable local activity here, so much so in Winterton that two rival beach companies existed – the 'Young Uns' and the 'Old Uns'. Their enmity drove rifts into families. The 'Young Uns' were devout Methodists, and met in a shed, or 'court', on a sand hill just north of the Parish Gap. The famous local resident Joseph Hume persuaded the companies to unite but resentments muttered on, gradually giving way to an even stronger anti-Sea Palling feeling. Winterton fishermen would hardly dare come ashore in that nearby village.

Sea sandwort is a small plant but one which colonises sand just above the high water mark and assists dune-building.

The tower of Winterton's church of the Holy Trinity is 132 feet high and it is claimed that on the proverbial 'clear day', the spire of Norwich Cathedral can be seen. Inside the church, a most unusual Fishermen's Corner has been created as a tribute to those who have lost their lives over the years. All the objects have direct connections with the sea. The cross is made from ships' timbers and the 'ship' lamp is in memory of a former verger. The flag was presented by the then Prince of Wales (later Edward VIII) in 1932, and ropes and nets make up the background. Appropriately, close to this tribute corner are rescue boards listing the deeds of Winterton's lifeboatmen. The first Winterton RNLI boat was stationed here back in 1858.

Water-filled 'dune slacks' are ideal for the rare natterjack toad.

Winterton Dunes extending for more than 250 acres are probably the second largest area of dunes in the country. Lucky visitors may see kestrels, warblers, chiffchaff and larks. Little terns nest in the shingle and this area is regarded as one of the most important areas for this species. In addition it is very important for the rare natterjack toad, whose distinguishing feature is the yellow stripe down its back. The pools within the dune hollows

Ancient and modern: Somerton wind farm and Winterton church.

Winterton's 'rondavels' at the Hermanus Holiday Centre are a reminder of South Africa.

provide an ideal habitat and where areas have dried out, similar conditions have now been created for the toad population.

Hemsby and Scratby are close neighbours, offering the bright lights of a seaside holiday in the Yarmouth mould, catering for all ages. Hemsby has grown into a large and very popular resort, and its population can increase 8 times during the summer. Its name is probably of Norse origin, meaning the home or farm of one 'Hem', and it has a Domesday pedigree, listed as a hamlet of 43 meadow acres and 50 households. It had 2 salt-pans and 160 sheep. The church of St Mary the Virgin which we see today is 14th century. Just after the end of the last war, with rationing still in place, the villagers had the bonus of free fruit when a ship struck the dangerous Scroby Sands and had to abandon its cargo of oranges.

Hemsby, and this area in general, was badly hit by the 1953 floods, with a great deal of damage caused, and the sea is still a considerable threat. When the tide is at a particular level, 'scouring' takes place and interesting features emerge along the shoreline. In Hemsby the remains of a Stirling bomber emerged in 1971, and at other times ancient ships' timbers have been exposed.

Scratby like its close neighbour Hemsby offers all the pleasures of the seaside, exploring the dunes for example, but with plenty to enjoy if the weather is inclement.

A fitting tribute in Winterton church to local fishermen.

An interesting use for an old boat at Winterton.

Hemsby provides popular holiday entertainment for everyone.

JOSEPH HUME (1777-1855)

The political philosopher Joseph Hume lived near Winterton. In his young days he was a Surgeon in the East India Company. By the age of 30 he had made his fortune and for the next 30 years was at the centre of political affairs, particularly as a campaigner against abuses. For example it was largely due to his efforts that flogging in the army, press gangs and imprisonment for debt (Mr Micawber's syndrome) were abolished. His watchword was 'Peace and Reform'. He also started the Savings Bank movement, and his daughter Eliza Greenhow (who has a memorial in Winterton church) is remembered for the splendid work she did in the 'National Schools' movement. Hume purchased Burnley House in East Somerton (formerly Somerton House).

The politician, Joseph Hume, died at Burnley Hall in 1855.

THINGS TO DO

❶ **Church of the Holy Trinity**, Winterton: explore this splendid flint church observing the knapped flintwork as you enter. Inside the church look out for the fishermen's corner, the memorial to Joseph Hume and another to his daughter Eliza Greenhow; look out also for the memorial to a former Rector, Revd. Porter who died whilst trying to save a choirboy from drowning in 1932

❷ **Walk:** explore the large area of Winterton's dunes or those at Hemsby and Scratby. Take care not to damage fauna and flora. In Winterton look out for the unusual 'rondavels'.

❸ **A touch of red:** as you turn off the main coast road for Scratby beach, look out for the collection of telephone boxes and pillar boxes. Mr Keith Lawson is the collector. He also runs an amazing antique clock shop, with a thousand clocks on display.

❹ **Pubs and eating places:** The Fisherman's Return (01493 393305), Winterton is a 300 year-old brick and flint pub; Lacon Arms (01493 730806), and King's Head (01493 730568), Hemsby.

❺ **'Worth a detour':** The California Tavern (01493 730340), California (1875).

A 'museum' of pillar boxes and old telephone kiosks at Scratby.

24 – Caister-on-Sea

He who fights and runs away, lives to fight another day!
(Sir John Fastolfe)

The word Caister comes from the same Latin root as 'Chester', 'Castor' or 'Caster'. and of course means 'castle'. The land to the north-west, west and south-west of Caister was, in Roman times, intersected by inlets of the sea. The area covered was what we now know as Broadland and was connected to the sea in two places; to the north there was a large river mouth between Happisburgh and Hemsby and to the south another where Yarmouth is today. Entering the river system at Yarmouth one would have direct water access to the area's premier town of Venta Icenorum, (Caistor St Edmunds near Norwich). To protect this route two fortifications were built, one in the north at Caister and the other on the south side at Burgh Castle. The remains of the former are visible, though not as extensive as those at Burgh Castle. Protection was needed against raiding hordes of Saxons. Caister became a port and it has been said that it was the only port in Britain at that time handling cargoes of wine, glassware and pottery, mainly imported from the Rhineland.

Caister has fine sandy beaches but, like the rest of the Norfolk coast, it has suffered from erosion. Up until the mid 16th century a spit of land extended eastwards, known as Caister Ness. It then disappeared. But of course coastal erosion has continued over the centuries. In 1793 a new Manor House was built, which in the 19th became a hotel and golf course. In 1941 this started to slip into the sea and in subsequent years more and more was swept away; today nothing remains. This emphasises the fragile nature of the east Norfolk coastline which continues to change dramatically.

As a resort Caister-on-Sea is quieter than its livelier neighbour Great Yarmouth. The town caters for family holidays of every kind with plentiful entertainment. To the south-east there is a large sandbank called Scroby Sands. On this sandbank are some thirty wind-powered generators and they produce enough electricity to meet the energy demands of 40,000 homes.

Caister Castle was the home of Sir John Fastolfe, the original for Shakespeare's Falstaff.

Hemsby to Hopton

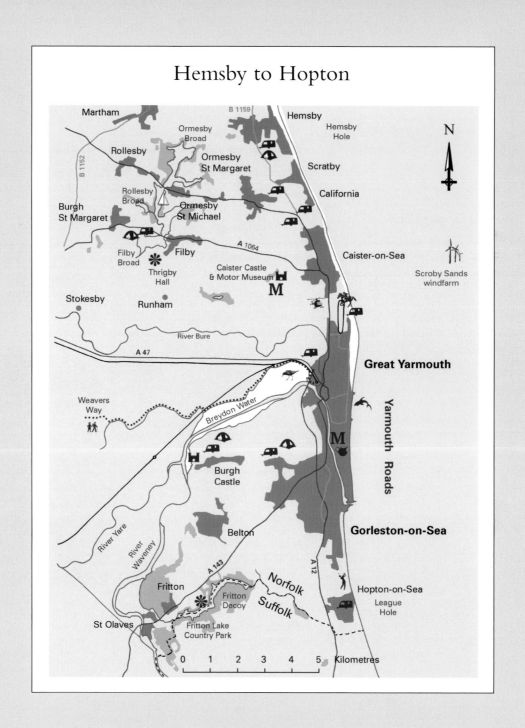

At the beach car park you will see the two lifeboat houses. A lifeboat was first placed at Caister in 1845 although the Caister Beach Company had been using boats for rescue since 1791. In 1857 the RNLI took over responsibility for all lifeboats. Caister was the last station in East Anglia to use a sailing lifeboat and in 1941 gained its first motor boat. In 1969 the RNLI decided to close the station. There was public outcry as Caister held the record for the most lives saved by any lifeboat station in the British Isles, a total of 1,814 persons. The motto of the Caister lifeboat service is 'Caister men never turn back' so, true to this, the day after the RNLI closure the Caister Volunteer Rescue Service (now known as the Caister Volunteer Lifeboat Service) was set up. With the aid of such 'names' as Bernard Matthews, the Norfolk turkey farmer, and Jim Davidson the comedian, the Caister crew are able to continue their work and today have a 'state-of-the-art', Dutch KNRM vessel propelled by water jets instead of the conventional screws.

Marram grass thrives when covered by wind-blown sand and allows sand dunes to build up.

The sparse remains of this once important Roman fort.

Caister's old and new lifeboat houses.

The snow bunting is a winter visitor to North Sea coasts. Because of the large amount of white in the plumage , they are sometimes called 'snowflakes'.

One mile west of Caister is Caister Castle. It was built in 1432 by Sir John Fastolfe after his return from Agincourt. To build a castle one had to have a 'License to Crenellate'. Fastolf must have fought well at Agincourt as King Henry VI (1422-1460) only granted five such licenses in his reign. Fastolfe was the model for Shakespeare's Falstaff in his play 'Henry IV'. After his death the castle passed into the hands of the Paston family (see p.113). The castle was positioned on the site of a former manor house and is built of brick. As such it could not have survived sustained attack. It was more of a defensible manor house. There was a siege in 1469 led by the Duke of Norfolk, who claimed to be the rightful owner, against John Paston. The siege lasted five weeks before Norfolk won.

Today it houses a motor museum with the largest private collection of motor vehicles in Great Britain, including the first real motor car, an 1893 Panhard et Levassor.

THINGS TO DO

❶ **Lifeboat sheds:** (01493 722001); open to view current lifeboats and also lifeboat memorabilia.

❷ **Caister Roman Fort:** remains of defensive wall, gateway and buildings. Managed by English Heritage (01223 582700).

❸ **Caister Castle** (01572 787251): ruin of a brick castle; connection with the Paston family now houses a motor museum.

❹ **Pubs and eating places:** Kings Arms (01493 720648); Old Hall (01493 720400); The Ship Inn (01493 728008); there are also many fish and chip shops, small cafes and restaurants in the centre of the village.

25 – Great Yarmouth, Gorleston-on-Sea and Hopton-on-Sea

Upon the whole, the finest place in the universe.
(A description of Great Yarmouth by Peggotty from *David Copperfield*)

Pegotty's Great Yarmouth, with its boathouses on the beach, was very differnt from the town that exists today. In Dickens' day Great Yarmouth (the locals drop the 'Great') was a port and fishing town with links to the continent and other British ports via the North Sea. Its trade reached far inland via the network of rivers throughout east Norfolk. Indeed the area has been of importance for maritime trade since Roman times. At that period there was a large estuary with a small sand and shingle island at the mouth. Over time this island increased in size due to the deposit of sediment stable enough for a walled town to be created. It gradually became inhabited and Great Yarmouth emerged. Yarmouth's North Beach has built up by about a quarter of a mile since World War II, its dunes providing a supported bird sanctuary.

Over time it became the centre of the herring fishing industry. The coming of the railways and the Victorian passion for the sea and its bracing air changed Yarmouth into a resort. In its heyday there were three railway stations catering for the day trippers and those staying longer. The stations were Yarmouth Vauxhall, Beach and Southtown; of these only the Vauxhall station remains. Yarmouth soon became a popular holiday destination for the folk from the Midlands and London; at weekends in the summer dozens of excursion trains and a large number of motor coaches would come to the town.

Today the sea-front has amusement arcades, a theatre, a circus, and at the southern end a Pleasure Beach. There are fish stalls, rock and candy floss shops, doughnut outlets and the usual fish and chip stands. It is very much like Blackpool without the trams and the tower! There are five miles of good sandy beaches and hotels and boarding houses adorn the sea-front and the streets behind. Two piers were built to cater for visitors. Wellington pier opened in 1854 and Britannia pier in 1858. Today Britannia pier hosts summer shows which over the years have starred some of Britain's top entertainers. There are pleasure gardens where once the sober Victorians would walk and take the air.

The tower is part of the town walls, the most extensive of any town in the country.

Yarmouth's 18th century fishermen's 'hospital', almshouses in effect for needy sailors and fishermen. A fine building with many interesting features.

The glitzy advertisements for Yarmouth's summer shows on the Britannia pier.

The glitzy advertisements for Yarmouth's summer shows on the Britannia pier.

A hardy family braving the spring breezes.

Fishing, especially for herring, has been important since the 11th century. After the Norman Conquest the fishing fleet increased dramatically. Fishermen came from all over Britain and beyond to settle and work in Yarmouth. A Herring Fair was held each autumn and this attracted hundreds of boats from all parts of Europe. The fish became known as 'the silver darlings' and by the beginning of the 20th century the average annual catch was about five hundred and thirty million fish. The herring was found in large numbers each autumn in the North Sea and the merchants who sold the fish became very wealthy. One of the reasons why the herring made so much money was because they could be easily preserved, either by smoking or salting. Herrings which are cleaned, split and smoked are called 'kippers' and those remaining unsplit are known as 'bloaters'. At one time it was said that one could walk from Yarmouth to Gorleston across the herring-boats crowded in the harbour. Now no large drifters or trawlers ply their trade from Yarmouth. The port has however, provided a necessary sea-link with the off-shore North Sea oil industry. Today only a few rig-supply ships use the port, and other shipping, for example the trade with Europe and Scandinavia, has also dwindled. Now it is unusual to see large ships in the port at South Quay. Modern Yarmouth relies heavily on the tourist trade.

The old town of Yarmouth is sandwiched between the 'glitzy' sea-front and the port on the banks of the River Yare. Here is a flourishing commercial centre with good shops and a regular market. Yarmouth's medieval town walls are one of the most complete in the country. It was in 1261 that King Henry III granted Yarmouth the right to build a

Yarmouth's fine parish church of St Nicholas was almost destroyed by fire bombs.

town wall. The last time they were prepared for use 'in anger' was at the time of the Spanish Armada in 1588. The river protected the western flank of the town and the walls with their eighteen towers protected the remainder.

The parish church of St Nicholas was founded by the first bishop of Norwich, Herbert de Losinga, and consecrated in 1119. It is cruciform in shape with a central tower and has seen many changes over the centuries. The nave was rebuilt in the reign of King John and the west front with its towers and pinnacles was constructed between 1330-1338. The church at one time contained eighteen chapels and these were maintained by merchant guilds or private families. During the Commonwealth the Independents appropriated the chancel, the Presbyterians the north aisle and the Anglicans used the rest of the building. Brick walls were erected to separate these areas and these remained in place until the 19th century. During the Second World War Yarmouth was badly bombed; the church took a direct hit and was gutted by fire. Rebuilding took place after the war and it is one of the largest parish churches in the country.

The old town plan was of four main streets running north to south interconnected by narrow alleyways. These alleys, of which there were about 145, became known as 'the rows'. They are as narrow as one metre in width; many were paved with pebbles, or more rarely, flagstones. In the area of the rows there were over three thousand houses bordering the alleyways with an estimated fifteen thousand people living there. This is where the fisher folk lived and where they carried out their various trades, in the smoke houses for example. Imagine the smell on a hot day with the fish, smoke and open drains 'flavouring' the atmosphere! It is said that they were built east to west so that the strong easterly winds and rain could clear the smell away. To get provisions around the rows and to move goods from the harbour to various parts of the town, a special cart known as a 'troll cart' was used. It was about twelve feet long with two wheels under one end. It was narrow enough to get up and down the rows, unless you met another coming the other way. The poor sanitation and open gutters spread disease and in 1349 the Black Death reduced the population by more than seven thousand. In Napoleonic times the rows were an ideal hunting ground for the Press Gangs. During World War II many of the rows were destroyed by air raids, and since then others have been pulled down to make way for new developments. Of those that survive many are simply alleyways connecting the main streets, but signs of the past are still there. Each row is still numbered and the appearance of some is still authentic.

One of the rows in Yarmouth's old town.

The East Anglian coast has always been regarded as vulnerable to attack and Yarmouth has played an important role in defending this part of the country since medieval times. The town supplied ships and men for the Battle of Sluys in 1340, the first great English triumph at sea. Later it played a large part in the Battle of Calais in 1347 and because of this support, was rewarded by having its coat of arms halved with the Royal coat of arms. At the time of the Civil War the last person to sign King Charles' death warrant was the town's MP, Miles Corbet, who lived in a house on the Market Place. After the Puritans were ousted from power by Charles II at the restoration, Corbet was hounded and had to flee from Britain. He was tracked down to Holland and brought back to the Tower of London where he suffered a grisly end.

Yarmouth's coat of arms appropriately includes herrings.

A day out at the races is always popular.

ANNA SEWELL (1820-1878)

Anna Sewell, the author of 'Black Beauty', was born in a 17th century house on Church Plain. The house is now a museum. At the age of fourteen she fell while walking home from school in the rain, injuring both ankles. She became lame for the rest of her life, possibly through incorrect treatment for her injury, and was unable to walk or stand for any length of time. She never married and remained living at home with her parents. By 1871 her health was declining and it was at this time she wrote her famous book encouraging those who worked with horses to treat them with kindness and sympathy. Her family were now living at Catton near Norwich and her mother wrote whilst Anna dictated. She sold the novel to the publishers Jarrold and Sons for forty pounds. It is said to be the sixth best-seller in the English language. Anna died of hepatitis just five months after its publication. She was buried on 30th April 1878 in the Quaker burial ground at Lammas near Norwich. It is now the garden of a private house but the gravestone can be seen in the garden wall.

A fitting memorial to the nation's most famous sailor, who knew Yarmouth well.

Yarmouth's port is still very active, even if the herring drifters are no longer there.

At the time of the Napoleonic Wars Yarmouth was an important naval base. Military buildings also sprang up and one of the most important was the Naval Hospital. Originally it catered for those wounded during the Napoleonic Wars but it later became a barracks. Some years later it reverted to being a hospital specialising in mental illness in the navy. The sailors' naval slang for mental illness is still 'going to Yarmouth'. In 1702 the corporation built a 'hospital', (really almshouses,) for 'decayed' fishermen and it is situated at the north-eastern corner of the market place.

Admiral Lord Nelson often used Yarmouth when setting sail or returning from a voyage. He arrived here in 1800 after the Battle of the Nile. He was given a hero's welcome and the crowd carried him to the 'Wrestler's Inn' on Church Plain and there he was presented with the 'freedom of the borough'. Legend has it that when the town clerk was administering the oath he noticed that Nelson's left hand was placed on the bible. He exclaimed, 'Your right hand, my Lord!' 'That,' replied Nelson curtly, 'is in Tenerife!' Following Nelson's death at Trafalgar in 1805 an appeal was launched in the town to raise funds for a fitting memorial. The money was raised and in 1819 a column was completed on the South Denes in his memory. The column is topped with a statue of Britannia which is not facing out to sea but rather towards Nelson's birthplace of Burnham Thorpe. This column appeared some thirty years before the one in Trafalgar Square in London and at a height of 144 feet is only a few feet shorter. It has been restored to commemorate the bicentenary of Nelson's death.

Yarmouth is linked to the Broads via the three rivers which flow into the sea here, the rivers Yare, Bure and Waveney. The confluence of the Yare and the Waveney occurs at the west end of Breydon Water, a vast expanse of mainly shallow water about five kilometres in length. Those who navigate it have to take great care. There is a nature reserve here which is managed by the RSPB. Large numbers of migratory birds pass through in spring and autumn. Among the many species which can be seen are cormorant, sandwich tern, oystercatcher, redshank, dunlin, curlew, shelduck and little grebe.

Across the River Yare and to the south west is the town of Gorleston-on-Sea. Throughout many years of Yarmouth's importance Gorleston was only a small village and, as with so many seaside settlements, it was the coming of the railway that led to the growth of the town. The railway line to Yarmouth from Lowestoft and the south passed through Gorleston, so a station was built.

Gorleston has fine, sandy beaches which nestle below low cliffs. Gorleston has its own 'bay' at the north end of the beach and it formed in the lee of the long breakwater which marks the entrance to Yarmouth harbour and provides a safe, sandy area for bathing. The various marine activities include wind surfing, yachting and jet-skiing. From the cliffs there is a panoramic view over Yarmouth harbour in the north to the cliffs at Corton in Suffolk in the south. The town offers other attractions and entertainments. The resort has its own theatre, the Gorleston Pavilion, an Edwardian theatre and a listed building. The capacity is three hundred, with the audience sitting at candlelit tables for the various performances. The 'Ocean Rooms' are Gorleston's own nightspot. Gorleston is quieter and less brash than its 'big brother', Yarmouth.

Both the black-tailed godwit (above) and the bar-tailed godwit can be seen at Breydon. Locally, the 12th May is sometimes called 'godwit day'.

The Pavilion Theatre, Gorleston.

The east wall of the Roman fort of Gariannonum.

Fennel was probably introduced by the Romans. It thrives in dry places near the sea.

The village of Burgh Castle (Burgh means a fortified place) today lies about 2 miles inland from the coast. It lies off the A12 to the west of Yarmouth and Gorleston, at the southern end of Breydon Water. Although not on the coast it is included because of its historical importance.

The modern village lies along the minor road which leads from Gorleston. There is a mixture of old and modern buildings and they are typical of the area. There are the remains of a local brickworks on private land, and many of the older houses contain bricks which have 'Burgh Castle' stamped on them. At the point where the road from Gorleston turns sharp to the south (to avoid the River Waveney) stands the round-towered church of St Peter & St Paul and the remains of the Roman Fort of Gariannonum.

What is now Breydon Water and the valley of the rivers Yare and Waveney, 2000 years ago was a large inlet of the sea. The fort was possibly built in the early 4th century to guard (together with its related fort at Caister on the northern flank of the estuary) the river routes inland west to Venta Icenorum (Caistor St Edmund near Norwich) and north-west to the industrial complex at Brampton near Aylsham. It was common then for raiders to come by sea from Scandinavia and northern Germany. The fort, of brick and flint construction, is large and covers about six acres. The walls still stand to a height of over 12 feet and exist on three sides. The fourth, west wall, has been lost to river erosion. The east wall has four large, round bastions which may have had ballistae mounted on the top. The main gate is also in the east wall. The other walls had postern gates. The personnel occupying the fort were a cavalry unit. This is a place of peace and quiet and the view to the west is ideal for watching the birds, especially wildfowl, which inhabit the marshes and rivers of Broadland.

Hopton-on-sea is the last coastal village, heading south, in Norfolk. It lies about five miles south of Gt Yarmouth. It is a small village made up of mainly 20th century housing and a large holiday complex. Potter's Holiday Village is the only 'five star' holiday village in England. It is the home of the International Indoor Bowls Champion-ships and also has a health centre, golf course, swimming pools and West End style shows. The beach is a clean, wide, sandy strand, flanked by low cliffs on the landward side. There is plenty of room, even if Potter's has its full quota of 600+ people staying in the cara-vans. It is best to park any vehicle in the village and then walk to the beach. Beach Road is a narrow lane which ends at the top of the cliff and there is no parking space at the end and little room to turn a vehicle.

Hopton beach towards Gorleston.

The original parish church is a ruin and signs are in place warning people to stay clear of the building. There is a fence all round. No doubt on moonlit nights it can seem a 'spooky' place and there are indeed ghost stories about Hopton. Several instances are recorded of motorists on the A12 suddenly seeing a person, dressed in a large hat and wearing a long coat with old fashioned, long-laced boots on the feet coming towards them. Despite braking and swerving they invariably pass through the macabre figure, very often finishing on the verge or in a ditch. Getting out of the vehicle they can find no trace of anyone!

River Waveney near Burgh Castle.

1 The Golden Mile: explore Yarmouth's seafront, amusements, shops, stalls, gardens. Seal trips to Scraby Sands.

2 St Nicholas' Church: largest parish church in England.

3 The Nelson Monument: open to the public after restoration.

4 Sea-Life, (01493 330631) Marine Parade: view marine creatures close up, everything from sharks to seahorses.

5 Hippodrome Circus, (01493 844172) just off Marine Parade: circus with 'PC' acts. Good fun for young and old.

6 Museums: 'Time & Tide' (01493 743930) the story of Gt Yarmouth; 'Tolhouse Museum' (01493 745549) tells of crime & punishment in Yarmouth; 'Row 111, Old Merchants' House & Greyfriars Cloisters' (01493 875900) the sights & sounds of the Yarmouth of yesteryear; 'Elizabethan House' (01493 855746) domestic life from Tudor to Victorian times; 'Norfolk Nelson Museum' 01493 850698) story of Nelson's life and times; 'Town Hall' (01493846345) magnificent civic building. Group tours only, must be prebooked.

Sunset over Breydon Water. Its waters are salty and tidal. It provides a peaceful refuge from the bustle of Yarmouth.

7 Exhibition Galleries: exhibits from Yarmouth museum's art collection (01493 857900).

8 Pavilion Theatre, Gorleston: Edwardian theatre with live shows (01493 662832).

9 Burgh Castle: Romano-British fort. Free entry. Approach from Gorleston.

10 Walks: There are guided walks around Yarmouth (01493 846345). There are also easy walks along the promenades or beaches.

11 Pubs and eating places: Yarmouth; The Wrestler's Inn (07743 388979), has Nelson connections; The Mariners Tavern, (01493 332299); The Red Herring,(01493 853384); The Two-necked Swan, (01493 331121); The Gallon Pot (01493 842230); there are endless good pubs to choose from in Yarmouth – or if you are stuck, chips on the prom!

12 TIC: Marine Parade, Great Yarmouth (01493 842195).